Contact Improvisati

For Keriac.
With heartfelt thanks for her inspiration and challenge.

Thomas Kaltenbrunner

Contact Improvisation
moving, dancing, interaction

With an introduction to New Dance

Meyer & Meyer Publishing

Die Deutsche Bibliothek – CIP Einheitsaufnahme

Kaltenbrunner, Thomas
Contact Improvisation : moving – dancing – interaction / Thomas
Kaltenbrunner. Transl. by Nick Procyk.
– Aachen : Meyer und Meyer, 1998
Dt. Ausg. u.d.T.: Kaltenbrunner, Thomas: Contact Improvisation
ISBN 3-89124-485-1

© 1998 by Meyer & Meyer Verlag, Aachen (Germany)
Olten (CH), Wien (A), Oxford (GB), Québec (CDN),
Lansing/ Michigan (USA), Findon/ Adelaide (AUS),
Auckland (NZ), Sandton/ Johannisburg (ZA)
Cover photo: Lutz Pape, Fotostudio Overlook, Braunschweig
Photos and illustrations see captions in the text, all reminding photos:
Lutz Pape, Fotostudio Overlook, D-Braunschweig
Illustrations: Brigitte Zeeh
Translation: Nick Procyk
Cover design: Walter J. Neumann N&N Design-Studio, Aachen
Cover exposure: frw, Reiner Wahlen, Aachen
Setting: Typeline, Dagmar Schmitz, Aachen
Printed by Burg Verlag & Druck, Gastinger GmbH & Co. KG, Stolberg
ISBN 3-89124-485-1
Printed in Germany

CONTENTS

II PRAXIS

Acknowledgements

First of all, many thanks to Nick Procyk for his translation. This book came about after my two-year full time training with Keriac – it was a great time; with teachers such as Scott Wells and Barbara Dilley and innumerable Jams. It reflects my own experience of Contact Improvisation and my own development as well.

I will say a few words about myself to give you the background to the book. I studied Psychology and "Naturheilkunde" in Germany and have worked for many years leading seminars in different aspects of Bodywork, communications training and have been teaching Contact since 1995. I have published two books arising from my work: "Shiatsu" and "Reflexology".

My motivation to take on this present book came mainly from three different sources: firstly it gave me an opportunity to reflect on my own positive experience within this dance form; secondly, a chance to introduce it to a wider audience and thirdly to strengthen the contact community.

This book arises out of my personal experience:
-   Material, which I have collected from many different sources, is simply handed on. A special thanks here to Keriac!
-   I have tried to present a broad overview of the wide (often unstructured) field of Contact Improvisation. Each teacher inherits a certain range of "classic" or "standard" material, (opinions about what this is differs of course!) and then proceeds to develop their own personal style and interpretation of what CI is about. This leads to great differences between teachers and teaching styles.
-   Making choices means setting limits and each choice is a result of personal experience and judgement.
-   Out of the vast range of exercises to be found in Contact workshops, I chose those which I find personally resonant and useful.
-   I would like to emphasise that this should not be seen as a book based around the individual styles of a few selected teachers. The detective work needed to find out from which teacher each exercise originated is practically impossible.

Many thanks to my "models" in the book: Thomas Brändle, Tanja Fölster, Jorg Haßmann (.......who is also on the front cover), Margarethe Hoppe and Andrea Kunz.

Many thanks as well to "Danceoholyx", the students of Keriac's 1994/95 programme, for a wonderful time together, loving support and on the practical side, for their notes made during the training.

Special thanks for Nancy Stark Smith for her truly generous support and to all the people who have made their photos available.

Maybe my book will inspire others to publish more CI stuff!

Thomas Kaltenbrunner, Marburg, February 1998

I THEORY

*Photo 1: Curt Siddall and Daniel Lepkoff, Berkeley Moving Arts, 1978
(Photo: David Minehart)*

A WHAT IS CONTACT IMPROVISATION?

Two young men in T-shirts and sweat pants, roll and slide on the floor, moving close to each other, in constant bodily contact but without consciously looking in each others eyes. Even though one is short and slim and the other taller and more heavily built, they move together smoothly and evenly, balanced and flowing, sometimes slower then faster with an apparent effortless lightness. They rise from the floor, circling close to each other in a seemingly random way, one man's shoulder glides down the other's back, head touches head, hips lean against legs and suddenly the big man is lying relaxed on the back of the other. His weight seems light, the man supporting is relaxed and stable. The man underneath moves slightly to one side, the other one slides slowly to the floor and curls himself up. The slighter of the two now follows and copies this movement and ends up sitting amiably on his partner's shoulder. They roll over each other on the floor. Surprising each other with quick or slow turns, twists and stops. Neither leads the dance. Then they are standing again, one bends his knees and jumps into the air, the other one reacts and by holding onto his partner's hips, lifts him higher and places him onto his shoulder. Dangling there, head towards the ground, almost weightless, he now slowly twists and spirals down his partner's body onto the floor, moving, rolling....

This or something similar is what Contact improvisation looks like. It could be two women, a woman and a man, all the possible variations of age, size and weight (see Novack in "Sharing the dance"). At the heart of the dance is the interplay between gravity, impulse and dynamic. The dance is with one or more partners.

The basis is a constant bodily contact through a shared, ever-shifting contact point or surface with a partner. Movements arise from what has just occurred, without previous agreement, but from an alert awareness of the moment. A movement flow which is attentive, immediate and (sometimes) adventurous can then emerge. Further characteristics of this shared dance are:

- *Movement develops from within:* a part of our awareness is continually directed inwards towards the body, perceiving the minute shifts of weight and reacting accordingly. Simultaneously, and this has often to be learnt, the dancer is mindful of the immediate environment and is ceaselessly integrating new perceptions and impulses into the dance.
- *Going with the Flow:* the free and continual movement flow is bound together with a constant alternation between an active giving-of-weight and a passive taking-of-weight. For instance the dancers can actively pull, push, lift or simply follow the energy flow and momentum, letting each movement lead unrestrictedly into the next.
- *Free Improvisation:* there is no set choreography. Duets, trios, solos or larger group sequences can arise. Elements such as spatial organisation, specific choreographic vocabulary or gesture are seldom consciously used. Nevertheless, through the dynamic of change and the emergence of distinct moods and qualities within the improvisation, a choreography of the moment surfaces.
- *Natural movement:* the dancers do not differentiate between "everyday movement" and "dance". They can also laugh, cough, scratch or watch each other, depending on the situation.
- *Proximity to the audience:* the audience normally sits very close to the performers and there is usually no clearly defined boundary between the

stage and the spectators. Speciallighting and decor are not used and the dancers normally wear light comfortable clothing. This set-up is also to be found in "Jams" (p.26).

Contact improvisation is a creative process which occurs when two or more people move in mutual support and play with the shifting collective equilibrium. Contact improvisation is influenced by Modern dance techniques, acrobatic components etc., but has its own characteristic movement principles (see chapter - Contact improvisation structure). As well as addressing the relationship between the skeleton, musculature and reflexes, Contact improvisation also looks at the interactions within the perceptual body, the body-mind organism. Through the direct experience and perception of dance, we can access new pathways to our selves and our environment. This is what could be called the contemplative aspect.

Contact — to be connected to your self, others and most importantly the space in-between!

Improvisation- letting the movement which comes from the moment of contact exist and permitting the adventure of "meeting in movement".

A few definitions:

"Just the pleasure of moving and the pleasure of using your body is, I think, maybe the main point. And the pleasure of dancing with somebody in an unplanned and spontaneous way, where you're free to invent and they're free to invent and you're neither one hampering the other - that's a very pleasant social form".[1]

Steve Paxton

Two people move together, in contact, maintaining a spontaneous physical dialogue through the kinaesthetic sensual signals of shared weight and common or counterpoised momentum. The body, in order to open to the sensations of momentum, weight, and balance, must learn to release excess muscular tension and abandon a certain amount of wilful volition to the natural flow of movement at hand. Skills such as rolling, falling, and being upside down are explored, guiding the body to an awareness of its own natural movement possibilities.[2]

Danny Lepkoff

11

Contact improvisation is an activity related to familiar duet forms such as the embrace, wrestling, martial arts, and the jitterbug, encompassing the range of movement from stillness to highly athletic. The exigencies of the form dictate a mode of movement which is relaxed, constantly aware and prepared, and on-flowing. As a basic focus, the dancers remain in physical touch, mutually supportive and innovative, meditating upon the physical laws relating to their masses: gravity, momentum, inertia and friction. They do not strive to achieve results, but rather, to meet the constantly changing physical reality with appropriate placement and energy. [3]

Steve Paxton

Contact improvisation is the beauty of natural movement combined with full communication. [4]

Curt Siddall

Contact improvisation is the way in, an attempt at a dance which abandons the normal forms and borders of dancing. It is a "game" between two or more people using moving and being moved: active, reactive, experimental, reciprocal, charged..... Contact improvisation is one of the physical languages to come out of Post-Modern-Dance. It is about communication via direct or indirect physical contact through a continually shifting point of bodily contact. Through this, an effortless flow of movement is created which leads to sometimes tranquil, sometimes animated improvisation. The dance reminds you of brawling, wild dances, children playing, lovemaking and of the gentler disciplines of Tai Chi or Aikido. [5]
   "Der Züricher Oberländer" from 11.11.1982 about a contact-workshop.

"Every time someone asks me "What is Contact improvisation?", my mind goes blank, even though I have carefully read and studied many written definitions of CI, trying to prepare this inevitable question. I invariably end up demonstrating physically. [6]

Keriac

1 HISTORICAL BACKGROUND

The history of twentieth-century dance can be described as a perpetual aesthetic revolution against stylised, perfectionistic dance-technique and performance. Contact improvisation has developed from the traditions of modern and post-modern dance into an autonomous form and is perhaps a new cry for freedom for the identity of dance.

1.1 Ausdruckstanz and Modern Dance

"The form, *in which modern dance expresses itself, is not haphazard, is not an unique creation of somebody's nor devised for any particular purpose but has grown out of the times we live in.*"[7]

Mary Wigmann

Around the turn of the century, European dancers turned away from the overemphasised technical perfection within classical ballet. They looked for opportunities to unite spiritual expression together with natural movement. It was about the communication of ideas and emotions and the pre-eminence of the individual within society. Closely tied to the term *"Ausdruckstanz"* are *Rudolf von Laban* (1879-1958) and *Mary Wigmann* (1886-1973). Reflected in Ausdruckstanz were an emancipated bodily awareness and a changed individual approach towards personal and artistic freedom. Free improvisation was discovered as a tool for choreography. The dance came from the body and not from the mind. Movements should be in tune with the given anatomy.

Modern dance had problems to find recognition in Germany. This was due on one hand to the dominance of classical ballet, and on the other to hindrance from the National Socialists and the outbreak of war. But this turning away from the *"aristocratic"* ballet was more or less constant in the USA. *Isadora Duncan* (1878-1927) approached such subjects as the influence of capitalism on the workers and used neither elaborate costume nor stage scenery. With regard to the dance technique of this period, emphasis was put onto the solar plexus, which was used as a place from which the movement impulses arose. *Martha Graham* (1894-1991), influenced by the ideas of *Sigmund Freud* and *C.G. Jung* concentrated more on psychological aspects, stories or dream-symbols. Her dances dealt not with outside realities but inner processes. She showed the mythical and symbolic side of humanity. Her dances stressed the pelvis as the centre which was, during this period, revolutionary and provocative.

Differences between modern dance and contact improvisation are clearly seen when considering *"falling"* and the consequent contrast in aesthetic standards: ballet and modern dance work with geometric centres; almost everything is based around the balanced torso and not "off centre". Contact improvisation works with the centre of gravity, the awareness of ones own weight, questioning how we can use this corporeal mass to move in space. This also includes of course, being above, below or next to the centre and continue moving. In contact improvisation we are invariably falling, which provokes fear, and therefore must know how to approach the floor, how to fall without hurting ourselves. Because of this risk of injury there are a lot of exercises based around "off centre" movement. Ballet is mostly about moving from the centre, whereas modern dance concentrates more on the diagonals in the body, which leads to a more dynamic dance form (see Practice section.). Limon technique focuses more on falling and recovery, falling towards the floor and using momentum to come upright again. Graham technique uses contraction and release, towards the centre and out again.

1.2 Post-modern Dance

Three examples will be used to look at post-modern dance:
Merce Cunningham, Anna Halprin and *Judson Church Dance Theatre.*

1.2.1 Merce Cunningham: the body as physical reality

"... I don't ever want a dancer to start thinking that a movement means something. That was what I really didn't like about working with Martha Graham - the idea that was always being given to you that a specific movement meant something specific."[8]

Merce Cunningham

Merce Cunningham (*1919), regarded as the most outstanding revitaliser of modern dance, began in the fifties to free the dance from the ossified aesthetics of Graham and Co. Movement should not mean anything anymore, rather be what it is - pure movement, nothing more and nothing less.

In his abstract choreographies, he eliminated all associations to the outside world, symbolic and material. There were no stories or definite ideas to be expressed. Cunningham did not want to create atmosphere, character, emotion or illusion. The dancers were not as individuals on stage; they did not present themselves, they only presented movements.

"Chance" replaced *"Reason"*. *Cunningham* used the laws of chance: for instance, a sequence of movement would be split up into short parts and by throwing a dice, a new sequence created. Or the dancers would be shown a few movements and then given five minutes to connect them up randomly. Through these processes, the audience was not "allowed" to develop any associations or discover meaning.

Sometimes *Cunningham* is included as one of the later representatives of Modern Dance. His technique reminds one of "modern", but his philosophy is more post-modern, therefore his inclusion in post-modern dance. Naturally, music, architecture and the visual arts all showed these post-modern concerns in an abundance ways.

1.2.2 Anna Halprin: Improvisation and Physical Theatre

"I imagine a future where many of us will call ourselves dancers and collaborate to make an art which concerns itself with primary areas of life ... for me, peace is a communal work process, a collective vision. The dance itself tries to exemplify a few of these methods in a truly grounded and practical way so that the people can say: yes, there are prospects of survival."[9]

Anna Halprin

Along with *Cunningham, Anna Halprin* (*1920) produced a powerful impetus for post-modern dance. In the fifties, she was working within the traditions of modern dance but later radically broke away and joined the provocative avant-garde revolving around *Grotowski* and the *Living Theatre*. She became interested in improvisation as a movement source and made it into a distinct and independent art form. The creative, non-judgemental process was the focus. Her aims in this body and movement work is to understand the nature of dance and to develop a natural, "authentic" dancer. She describes dance as "the art of bringing the emotional force in movement to expression" and speaks about a Life-Art-Process. Art gives impetus to daily life and daily life gives impetus to art. Halprin developed the "Movement Ritual", a flowing movement sequence in which the natural developmental stages from lying till standing and moving are reflected.

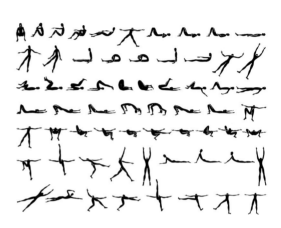

Figure 1:
(Designer Charlene Koonce;
with kind permission of
Anna Halprin)

Alongside of the personal, creative process, the private self, is the group process. Halprin's work created the RSVP model, a set of guidelines towards the creative process, which can be very helpful in making solo or group pieces. This model divides the creative process into four steps:

16

- *Resources:* collect and define the subject matter, motivation and aims to be worked with. Identify my sources. What material is there?

- *Score:* design a basic plan. A graphical representation of the process which leads finally to the performance. What is my plan?

- *Valueaction:* a word combined from "evaluation" and "action", which describes the active evaluation, analysis and decisions made over the course of the work process. What conclusions are to be drawn from my plan?

- *Performance:* the realisation and result of the ideas.

Halprin goes further than merely a recognition and sensing of the emotional content but expects an active participation. To act upon experience, creating a dance which has an intention, a theme. Her aim is not therapeutic but to deepen the experience of life and to form it artistically. She founded the *Tampala Institute* and summarises her work as an artistic contribution towards world peace. Through dance rituals *(e.g. Circle the Earth),* in which several hundred people can take part, she demonstrates the possibilities of breaking through deeply ingrained notions, the negative myths of conflict and war and the illusion of isolation.

A lot of these ideas found their way into contact improvisation through students of *Anna Halprin,* in particular her concept of performing. The performance often follows a *"score"*, which allows spontaneous decision making and change within the actual performance. Unlike a choreography, which is product-based, a score focuses on the process. The intention of a score, to be open *(open score)*, defines its quality. The avowed aim of these performances is a true encounter between performer and audience. *Halprin* observed how ever-increasing distance from traditional dance-theatre altered the role of actor and spectator. The reaction to an authentic presentation of real life situations releases the audience from the passive role of observer into an active participant of the event.

1.2.3 Experimental Dance-Theatre: Judson Church

"It included painters, musicians, poets, whole theater companies, individual dancers, dance companies ... there was in Judson itself definitely a scene in form and content."[10]

Steve Paxton

The beginning of post-modern dance is often linked to the founding in New York of the dance collective *Judson Dance Theatre* (1960 - 1964), which looked for ways to redefine dance. The dancers included *Steve Paxton, Trisha Brown, Yvonne Rainer, Judith Dunn, Lucinda Childs* and *Deborah Hay.* In contrast to *Cunningham,* they rejected structure and in particular, dance technique. They went one step further, jettisoned the traditional language of dance and used everyday, "pedestrian" movements such as sitting, lying, rolling, falling. Movements, which did not require a trained dancer, which everybody could do and perform. They also experimented with surreal ideas, disguised themselves in strange costumes or performed naked. Scope was given for collaboration between dancers and musicians, actors and artists and anybody who wanted could present their work.

The post-modern approach was not only to be seen in dance. There were similar developments within other art forms: Minimal Music, Action Painting, Minimal Art, Absurd Theatre and post-modern architecture.

1.3 New Dance

"My reverence for improvisational dance comes from those sacred moments in which I have felt forces deep within my body and psyche rise up together as partners. There is a feeling of humility and truth, and it is obvious what is to be done."[11]

Keriac

The aesthetic revolution taking place in dance was a little late in finding its way into Europe; it is normally identified under the term *"New Dance".* The phrase "New Dance" first appeared in England in the early seventies when a group of experimental dancers from *X6* in London published a magazine called "New Dance Magazine".

18

New Dance is a broad term, used mainly in Europe and less in the USA, encompassing many different approaches. It is seen as a further development leading to a fusion of various dance technique with improvisation - but leaving plenty of scope for other elements : dance-theatre, bodywork such as Alexander Technique, Feldenkrais, Release and further techniques involving "Body-Awareness-Work". In post-modern dance the pieces were often without a specific "content", mainly abstract but New Dance permits the use of personal material, bringing back the connection with the real world. For a New Dance workshop the dancer *Lilo Stahl* wrote: "New Dance technique is based around the interplay between tension and release in the body and focuses on finding the minimal energy needs in movement. The technique is oriented around a minimal physical training and through internal bodywork, promotes awareness / recognition of movement sources and associations. The connection with the fundamental techniques of the dance come through individual experimentation with specific movement impulses.... the Technique is used as support to extend the individual movement vocabulary and to break through entrenched movement patterns."

Important principles of New Dance are:
- Each individual is unique in their movement potential
- Sources for movement are to be found within the body.
- Awareness is directed inside the body and looks for the minimal energy pathways for movement
- Follow spontaneous movement impulses and overcome individual movement clich.
- Improvisation means: the discovery and creative use of personal movement material.
- Improvisation is a distinct and independent form for performance and can create affiliation to other art forms.
- Dance expresses an holistic view of the person, shaped through individual experience.
- New Dance choreographs the ordinary.

Dance has been, so to speak, democratised : dancing has rid itself of the aristocratic attitude (professional v. amateur) and from extreme physical demands. Dance is judged not by its technical perfection but by its ability to communicate, the tangible bond between performer and audience.

Seemingly rather vague, the term New Dance achieves a clearer definition through the personal subject matter of the dancers, workshop leaders and choreographers. Though a few have declared themselves to be *"New Dancers"*, it turns out after a closer examination of their work that they are really post-modern or experimental dancers. Similarly, people teaching New Dance as if it were ballet, gives the students a totally different picture of self, with far reaching consequences towards an assessment of New Dance and contact improvisation: why do a lot of people believe that in order to dance well they first have to become better? Why do many teachers fail to communicate the value of genuine and sincere self-expression?

Creative self-expression through dance should not be a territory solely and defensively occupied by professional dancers; everyone is a dancer! The pleasure to be found in dancing and a pride in one's own movement should be the sole criteria - and not physical achievement and technical perfection.

In its connection with (daily) life dance reveals its real vitality as an art form - as *Danny Lepkoff* knows from own experience: *"I remember feeling literally transported to another world when dancing, a world in which I was able to become a stronger self than I lived with day to day ..... the realm of contact improvisation I realised was not "dance" but living, the forces at play between two people dancing are those forces which exist day to day, ...I was left with the ever present challenge to realise my strong self in day to day living as well as the responsibility of achieving a healthy and true communion with those people I meet day to day."*[12]

New Dance, looked at broadly, is a further development and synthesis of various dance techniques with improvisation, bodywork, and movement forms. Contact improvisation is a distinct and separate part of this cultural abundance, absorbing ideas and impulses and producing new ones. There are interesting transfers between contact improvisation and ballet for instance.

2 The development of Contact Improvisation

2.1 Steve Paxton

"Contractive energy or tensions overpower the sensing of subtle movement, and so gravity is masked."[13]

Steve Paxton

The person regarded as the founder and initiator of contact improvisation is Steve Paxton. He began his dance training at **Connecticut College** in 1958 when he was 19. The teachers at that time included *Martha Graham, Jose Limon, Doris Humphrey* and *Merce Cunningham.*

When dancing for Cunningham, Paxton became critical of the hierarchical social structures within the company. The dictatorships and star systems were in stark contrast to the ideas of *Isadora Duncan* and *Laban,* whose work had promised freedom and egalitarianism. Another criticism was the tendency towards vacuity within the high technical perfection, which left audiences watching such dance performances with the feeling that their own movement was not worth exploring.

Paxton began to make his own pieces during the time with *Cunningham.* He introduced "normal" movement such as walking into his choreographies, which was the beginning of his interest in nondance movement. It opened up for him a whole new area of exploration, enriching and expanding the dance vocabulary. He saw walking as a "sympathetic link" between performers and spectators; it is something that both have experienced. It left space for the dancer's own particular qualities and enabled a development of individual style. Moreover, walking cannot be judged to be good or bad.

Paxton was also participating in the composition classes given by *Robert Ellis Dunn* in Cunninghams studio. *Yvonne Rainer,* another of the participants initiated the *"Continuous Project Altered Daily",* a piece which included rehearsal as part of the performance. Special regard was given to the spontaneous unforeseen events and their consequences. Out of this *"Continuous Project"* came the free improvisation group Grand Union, which existed between 1970 and 1976. Belonging to this group were, among others: *Yvonne Rainer, Steve Paxton, David Gordon, Trisha Brown, Barbara Dilley, Douglas Dunn* and *Nancy Greene.* This dance collective extricated itself from normal structures and focussed on improvisation in

21

groups, duets or as a solo form. These open-ended improvisations could switch from dramatic, surreal situations through movement games to intimate conversations.

During a Grand Union residency at *Oberlin College,* Ohio in 1972, *Paxton* made "**Magnesium**", a piece in which eleven men threw themselves and each other into the air, collided, caught and fell onto the floor. They tried not to work with any "learned" dance vocabulary but simply from reflexes.

If the body is in a risk situation, reflexes are activated, minimising the danger of injury and enabling a safe escape. The dancing lasted about ten minutes with a few minutes of standing still at the end.

Encouraged by this experience, *Paxton* gathered a group of about 15 good "athletes" to further explore the potential and principles of communication first discerned in *"Magnesium".* This group worked on what they called "contact improvisation". The raw materials were the physical forces of gravity, *momentum,* the force produced when hurling someone around and the consequences of all these actions.

Photo 2: Daniel Lepkoff and Steve Paxton, Cunningham Studio, NYC 1977 (Photo: Stephen Petegorsky)

The results were shown for the first time in June 1972 at the *John Weber Gallery* in New York. Participants included: Tim Butler, Laura Chapman, Barbara (Dilley) Lloyd, Leon Felder, Mary Fulkerson, Tom Hast, Danny Lepkoff, Nita Little, Alice Lusterman, Steve Paxton, Mark Peterson, Curt Siddall, Emily Siege, Nancy Stark Smith, Nancy Topf, David Woodberry. *Paxton* wrote about this period: "When, in 1972, a group of dancers began work on Contact Improvisation, it was a study of the way communication was possible through touch.... the movement which resulted from contact improvising - a non-rationalised, intuitive movement leading to unforeseen phrasing, positions and gambits. Basic movement upon intimate communication was appealing to me, after years of technical modern training.

There was a lot of hard work within this well-disciplined group. In the beginning *Paxton* curbed the social communication forms such as talking or laughter; this dance broke the cultural taboo of touch and he wanted to avoid the circumvention of the physical situation through talking and laughter. Social behaviour is often employed as a distraction from the real feelings of fear, arousal or indignance. For *Paxton* it was about exploring physical phenomena; giving themselves permission to go into areas which

Photo 3: Steve Paxton und Nita Little, First ReUnion tour, 1975, Natural Dance Studio, Oakland, California (Photo: Edmund Shea)

invoked things of a social nature but without being obliged to deal with them on a social level. He also wanted to avoid the participants losing themselves in psychological dramas or sexual fantasies. The interest lay exclusively in the physical dialogue defined by the following questions:

- What occurs during physical contact and giving of weight?
- What happens when we jump upon, lift and carry each other ?
- How do I give weight to the floor?
- How can I utilise gravitational forces in movement?

Paxton invited to this initial gathering a diverse group of people to work together, bringing different areas of experience such as gymnastics, release, sports, dance etc. to act as movement sources. Whatever skills the participants had were put to use, illustrating the non- hierarchical methods of accepting the potential and abilities of each individual. This is perhaps why contact improvisation is not called "Steve Paxton Technique"!

Paxton was curious to see what kind of dance develops from such a non-hierarchical structure and consciously looked for something different from that based upon the traditional choreographer-dancer relationship.

Further influences came from the martial arts, in particular Aikido, Yoga and Tai Chi and their relevance within this newly created form were acknowledged. After one week of practice/ rehearsal in New York loft, the initial group performed contact Improvisation for 5 hours a day for a week at the John Weber Gallery. These were the first performances called "*Contact Improvisation*". Many hours of this practice and performance were videotaped, later made into a documentary video, "Chute". From this event came certain rules of practice to be investigated in the subsequent work. *Nancy Stark Smith* relates the following to many of the performances in early years: "*What happened, I think, was the sensations were transmitted to the audience. They would come out of the performances flushed and sweating, almost, and thrilled as if they had been doing it themselves ... To tell you the truth, I don't think there was one performance we did that wasn't very enthusiastically received. It was like we had offered something to people as a way of looking at the movement and a way of experiencing movement that was very new and healthy, very vital and life-supporting.*"[15]

2.2 The expansion of the "Contact Community"⎯⎯⎯⎯

The next year, 1973, saw a part of this group, (*Little, Smith, Siddall, Radler, Paxton*) go to California and perform Contact Improvisation on a tour they named:*"You Come We'll Show You What We Do"*. The performance framework was very informal; spectators sat on chairs and on the floor on the edge of the performance space, no special lighting or costumes. At the same time, the first classes in this new form began. In summer, Paxton travelled with a few "contacters" to Europe and the first performance took place at Attico Galero in Rome.

In 1975 a new group formed, ReUnion (*N. Little, C. Siddall, N. Stark Smith, S. Paxton*) which was the first pure contact improvisation company. Other groups formed and a contact-community developed.

Nancy Stark Smith and Contact Quarterly

Nancy Stark Smith was a sophomore at *Oberlin College* majoring in writing and dancing, when *Steve Paxton* came with the Grand Union for their January 1972 Residency. Originally trained as an athlete and gymnast, she began to dance and was choreograph at *Oberlin* with the *Oberlin Modern Dance Company*, in classical modern and post-modern styles, working with various choreo-graphers including *Twyla Tharp* and *Brenda Way*. Dance in America in the early 1970's offered a new opportunity to integrate her love

Photo 4: Steve Paxton und Nancy Stark Smith, 1980
(Photo: Stephen Petegorsky)

of the athleticism of sports with her interest in the arts. During the *Grand Union's* 1972 residency, *Nancy* studied and performed in the work of the company members. She was impressed and greatly moved by Steve's men's performance, *Magnesium,* and afterwards mentioned to him that if he ever worked like that with women she'd love to know about it. A few months later he called, inviting her to NYC for the rehearsals and first performance of contact improvisation. She continued to travel and work closely with Steve and others throughout the 1970's and into the 80's, performing, teaching and developing the work.

In 1975, *ReUnion* briefly considered trademarking the name of Contact Improvisation and authorising teachers, as they had heard of people picking up the work (beginning to do Contact) from seeing performances and getting seriously injured by practising it without the proper training. Preliminary papers were drawn up but never signed, as they decided instead to start a Newsletter to encourage communication within the work, inviting people into the dialogue rather than pushing them out. This newsletter continued to develop into what is now a biannual magazine, **Contact Quarterly – a vehicle for moving ideas,** (see appendix for address) edited by *Nancy Stark Smith* and *Lisa Nelson*. It contains not only articles about contact improvisation but other themes and topics relating to post-post-modern or New Dance.

Other important elements within the contact community for keeping up-to-date are the national newsletters (see appendix for addresses) and the regular holding of *Jams* (open Contact sessions without supervision) such as the Breitenbush, Harbin-Hot-Springs or in Europe the Black-Forest-Jam. Also important are the annual Contact Teacher's Conferences and festivals such as the West-Coast-Contact-Festival in San Francisco.

2.3 Developments, trends, open questions _____

Contact improvisation differs from all other dance forms: originally it was not taught as a technique. It was seen as an investigation, an adventure. This is something immensely valuable and should not be allowed to disappear, though unfortunately, this is exactly what seems to be happening in Europe at the moment.

There are, of course, as in every "culture", many offshoots and trends within the contact community, with new developments continually emerging. Areas being addressed nowadays include sexuality, emotion and therapeutic aspects of contact improvisation. *Danny Lepkoff* was already raising these issues in Contact Quarterly in 1988 with an article entitled "Questions not to ask" :[16]

Why is the aerial lift a signature of an accomplished contact dancer?

Why are complete beginners so beautiful to watch, and experienced Contact Improvisers often so boring?

Why is there a hierarchy of Contact skills?

Why were many of my advanced Contact students unconsciously resistant to learning?

Why can someone become advanced in a form based on communication?

Why do I expect to get "danced on" at Contact jams?

Why are Contact-based performances so devoid of vision and self-examination?

Why does the allure of gymnastic skills overshadow the exploration of making contact?

Why do experienced Contact dancers get frustrated with beginners?

Why does a form rooted in the senses give rise to a generic look, when life itself is so varied?

Why did I overhear an audience member say during a C.I. performance, "How can adults do all of that and not seem to feel anything?"

Meanwhile - Contact Improvisation celebrated its 25 year anniversary in 1997 - this dance form has found its way into many different areas of life: schools, further education, sport, professional dance companies, theatre, dance-therapy (see chapter D, p. 176 - Areas of application). But contact improvisation is not limited to specific fields, it is also proving attractive to people simply interested in movement, people who look for (and find) fun and exuberance in dance.

Contact improvisation, taken as a whole, is at the junction (or point of contact) of sport, dance and therapy and therefore has the chance to spur on each of these areas with new energy.

Photo 5: Karen Nelson, Andrew Harwood, Nancy Stark Smith und Alito
Alessi, 1990 (Foto: Bill Arnold)

2.4 Influences

2.4.1 Aikido and Zen-Buddhism

"A free spirit is reflected in free movement. Aikido movements are very fluid.
This is because they are primarily circular or spirallic in nature though there
is some linear movement involved. Circular movement is not only fluid but has
powerful energy."[17]

Leonard P. Cohen

Since the 1960's, eastern philosophy has been influencing the artistic
notion of the body. *Steve Paxton* studied Aikido and travelled to Japan.
It showed him ways of falling and rolling without injury, ways of
perceiving the energy-flow between people and of how two bodies can
approach each other without premeditation. A sensitivity towards the dual
energies of two distinct bodies can lead to the manifestation of a third
energy emerging during the shared dance. Aikido permits the body to
yield to its protective instincts, the innate responses to the environ-

ment. A determination to achieve, to get results, according to the eastern view, achieves nothing but disharmony with the life-energy source - Ki and hinders learning. Aikido also introduced ideas from Zen-Buddhism into contact improvisation:

- Situation and circumstance are accepted for what they are: nothing is to be forced
- Movement is determined not by will but rather in harmony with forces which reach outside the body, such as gravity or centripetal force.
- The centre of the body is the belly : a person is "grounded" when they have a stability with the ground / floor. An acceptance of the force of gravity not a struggle against it, as the balletic manner of lightness and levitation.
- only through the unity of mind and body can a person, or in this case, a dancer have a harmonious and inspirational dialogue with their surroundings.

Apart from Aikido, principles and elements of other forms added to contact improvisation; Yoga, Tai Chi, the south American martial art - Capoeira. Some contact dancers link contact improvisation directly with the martial arts, for instance *Hillel Kraus* in "Martial Dance".

2.4.2 Acrobatics and dance as Art-Sport

"The AMERICAN DANCE GUILD invites your participation in "DANCE AS ART SPORT", a movement conference which will explore topics and techniques in improvisation. ...Included will be dance forms and activities for elementary and high school students, adult beginners, athletes & the disabled, as well as a variety of material of interest to the trained dancer."[18]

From Contact Quarterly, 1979

Simone Forti came up with the term "Art-Sport" after seeing *Steve Paxton* and *Nancy Stark Smith* dancing Contact together. *Paxton* had, along with others of the first contacters, been trained in Gymnastics and acrobatics. The physicality to be seen sometimes in contact improvisation has its roots here. In 1980, a conference was held under the title *"Improvisation: Dance as Art-Sport"*. Originally planned purely as a contact improvisation conference, other dance forms working with improvisation were eventually included.

29

Photo 6: Steve Paxton and David Woodberry, San Francisco Museum of Modern Art, 1976, ReUnion (Foto: Uldis Ohaks)

This proximity to sporting activities is perhaps the most important doorway to the mainstream and has let contact improvisation find its way into schools and universities, prisons and sport-centres.

2.4.3 Relaxed tension through Release

"Release work helped people feel their own weight ... sensing weight: the weight of the arm, the weight of the head, the pelvis ... it was wonderful for dancing to return to a real experience of weight and to the floor."[19]

Nancy Topf

A method which started its development in the early 1960's in the USA, later became generally known as "Release work". The founders of this approach include *Joan Skinner, Marsha Paludan* and *Mary Fulkerson*. What evolved was a "kinaesthetic training form": the term "Release" comes from *Graham's*" contract - release"; if we pull our energy towards the centre and then let go, this impulse can lead to movement through space. Fundamental ideas of *Mabel Todd* and *Lulu Sweigard* were coupled with principles of bodily alignment from the Alexander Technique and combined with the use of anatomical images for movement. Release Technique concerns itself with the question: how is the thought " I want to stand" physically translated into the action of standing? Science has still not come up with a solution to this question of how this picture or image of standing is transferred into the body. What happens when thoughts become action?

Release Technique works with internal imagery and through a creative process leads to a different approach to this inquiry. Key aims of Release are:

1. multi-directional alignment of the skeleton.
2. different planes of balance
3. an autonomy of movement of the various body parts.
4. efficient movement with the minimum of energy expenditure.

"Proper" alignment and balance is not seen as a inert state but a dynamic process of adjustment and modification of weight placement in space. The basic idea is that posture should be effortless. Good posture is a active rather than a static process, the body is not rigid but relaxed, flexible, loose and is kept in balance using the most efficient energy pathways, in contrast to "stomach in - chest out".

Release was already being studied by many practitioners of contact improvisation and was integrated as a corporeal experience - an experience exclusive to the physical process, not to be reduced to its conceptual properties. Release shows itself in the soft, flowing and economical movement of Contact.

2.4.4 Body-Mind Centering (BMC)

"The interplay between our subconscious and consciousness is a continual exchange and always a two-way flow. Consciousness and the subconscious are a continuum of a mind. They are each other's shadows or supports in their movement and expression."[20]

Bonnie Bainbridge Cohen

31

Body-Mind Centering (BMC) is a comprehensive movement re-education form developed through many years of research by *Bonnie Bainbridge Cohen*. She began to study the movement and learning processes of children and developed her work using anatomical, psychological, physiological and developmental principles. The interdependence of these principles together with the different organic systems in the body has a direct influence on movement development. BMC enables an inner awareness of movement and leads to a sensibility of how the mind, through movement, communicates with the body.

There are two fundamental areas in BMC :

1. The study of movement development in infants
This process, which each and every one of us goes through, has great similarities with evolution in the animal kingdom, from the earliest vertebrates to the primates. Inherited reflexes together with neuromuscular patterns form an outline for the development of our movement and simultaneously our mental, emotional and creative orientation in the world. Studying this "developmental movement" is a effective way of unearthing movement and behavioural problems and through specific exercises, allows readjustment.

2. Intensive study of the different systems within the body.
Glands, organs, nerves, muscles, bones, fluids, sensory systems etc are closely studied. The functioning principles of each system and the relationship to the other systems is found. The study goes beyond a pure collection of anatomical facts and figures, through specific exercises direct physical experience of each system is attained. One of her students wrote: "in each system, its associated mental or mind aspect is to be found and clearly separated from the other systems. In the organs for instance; depths of emotion, our personal way of processing ideas and concepts; our bones, supportive, angular, levers and lines along which our thoughts can orient themselves; the fluid systems, the motion between positions and rhythms of stimulation and tranquillity."[21]

BMC, because of its emphasis of a holistic study of the "body-mind-spirit" and the sensory experience of the sources of movement, was soon integrated into the work of contact improvisation practitioners. The aspects of deep physical self-awareness and understanding to be found within BMC has had a strong influence on the development of contact improvisation.

Other methods such as Feldenkrais, Alexander Technique or Authentic Movement support certain aspects of contact improvisation: directing perception inwards to a kinaesthetic awareness, a smooth, efficient way of moving, supportive of the anatomical systems.

2.5 Contact Improvisation: embodiment of cultural values

Contact improvisation came out of the experimental atmosphere pervasive in the 60's and 70's. The young generation was searching for new ways of life and political rectitude. Flower-Power stressed community, equality and steered away from the norms of competition and subjugation.

From the beginning, contact improvisation was a collective pheno-menon. Contact dancers lived together and created a wide network of contacts and mutual support. Contact improvisation can be seen as a physical manifestation of the values and convictions of this generation. It could also explain the fascination and euphoria of some of the first audiences, who were seeing a palpable embodiment of something which was present in their lives.

Co-operation and communication instead of competition!
Through giving-of-weight and playing with balance, the dancers always had to find collective solutions and pathways. If one dancer tried to impose their will onto the other, the dance soon became tedious and eventually came to a standstill. A sensibility for the partner and communication are naturally opposed to ego-trips.

Equality and hierarchy!
Right from the start, *Steve Paxton* expected that the practitioners of this new dance form experimented with the existing elements. They should free themselves from any previous notions and be responsible for finding their own way through the process. The emancipation of the individual enabled

creative improvisation and movement diversity. The dominating role of the Teacher was to be replaced by mutual reciprocity. "the Dance is the Teacher". This way of teaching was and still is not usual within the dance world. If you are simultaneously teacher and student, there can be no social differences or hierarchy.

Teaching therefore meant not a presentation of technique to be copied but an invitation to participate in an experiment. The main teaching method was " here is the problem, let's work on it. It is an experiment, we make joint discoveries, there are no rights or wrongs and there are no ultimate solutions. This remains just as relevant even when one of the dancers has less experience in contact improvisation than the other!" From this background, open improvisational meetings took place: "jams".

After more than 25 years of development, there is naturally a immense pool of resources showing ways and solutions within contact improvisation which a teacher can pass on. Even so, or maybe precisely because of this, anyone joining in contact improvisation sessions, can produce wonderful dancing. *Nobody would*, as *Keriac* believes, *"correct them, perhaps, at most, say only; " if you do this or that, you won't injure yourself...*"[22]

Self-possession and shared dependency!
Everything in contact improvisation happens through requesting and expressing intent: somebody gives their weight and the other is free to decide if or how much to accept. There is no guarantee that your intentions, your wishes, will be fulfilled. Self-possession and deep awareness of "being" is deeply rooted in this dance form. Keriac writes:*"contact improvisation is a model for social behaviour. What is this social system? It really is a non-hierarchical notion, each person is equal and each one has total responsibility for themselves and their behaviour. We try not to save or prevent the other from falling or sliding but to offer surface area. You are aware and sensitive and present but you do not control what is happening. You give a freedom of choice for the simple reason that the other is capable of doing things as well.*"[23]

Contact improvisation is also a model for interdependence. It is not a one-sided dependence but it is not an completely autonomous relationship either. It is, as Keriac continues:*"the ideal love relationship, or work relationship. I want to be interdependent, apart from the Parent-Child relationship. The child has a right to be dependent on its parents for a while, but even here the child has to be given more and more independence as it grows older."*[24] To take responsibility for yourself, when it comes down to it, can mean a calculated request for help as well!

The taboo of touch is demolished!

To touch, to come into physical contact with a stranger was a revolutionary and perturbing challenge. Touch, in a social context had always had a particular meaning. There is a difference whether we shake hands in greeting or touch arms or shoulders. Contact improvisation allows touch, contact, feelings are allowed to be felt and expressed in the dance. But whatever happens in the dance is not carried over into any social consequences: *"After an exciting dance"*, as *Keriac* points out, *"you don't need to get married straight away!"*[25]

Contact improvisation is perhaps one of the few social situations where, in an atmosphere of trust, these social borders can be inquisitively approached and newly defined.

Figure 2:
Comic Sheeps

Sex roles vanish.

Duets in contact improvisation are not heterosexually bound, are not in anyway an expression of romantic love and do not imply any specific content or meaning. A short comparison with ballet points up these differences in gender roles quite clearly. In both forms the duet form is of central importance. In ballet, the duet is primarily a "Pas de deux": a man and a woman dance a representation of romantic love. The roles are clearly divided: the man is strong, steadfast and carries the woman. She graciously balances on one leg and is transported.

This convention is often reflected in the various solos: the man demonstrates his prowess with enormous leaps and turns while the woman shows her flexibility, speed and virtuosity with her legs. The ballet duet normally takes place stage front, directed towards the audience; it emphasises the bodily extremities (arms, legs, head) and vertical, controlled balance. The movement material to be seen in contact improvisation emphasises an inward focus, towards the centre of the body and an awareness of the movement process within the duet. In and out of balance and disorientation are the creative sources for the movement impulse. Teaching experience shows that the question of bodily weight is more of a mental problem: if a woman for instance, "thinks" that she cannot support so much weight and then tries it out, she is normally astounded how little exertion is required; or how a relatively powerful man is amazed how heavy a "light" woman can be (because he is using his muscles....).

The movement vocabulary; rolling, jumping, lifting, falling, is there for both sexes. In a Contact duet, the man as well as the woman has to be able to give and take weight, to support, to carry and to yield whenever the situation calls for it. There is no compulsion to do any of these things of course and the rejection of somebody's weight can be integrated into the dance as well! Each and every variation of the masculine and feminine body can dance a contact duet. Differences in size or weight normally play no role; because the root of stability lies not in muscular force but rather in an optimal alignment, a slight woman can carry a much stouter man.

Photo 7: B. Zeeh and T. Kaltenbrunner in "Hommage au coeur", 1995
(Photo: Tom Erikson)

As mentioned previously, gender differences play no role in contact improvisation. it promotes a development of a more complete spectrum of qualities. Men can learn to be gentle, soft and acquiescent. They can learn a new way of communication with both sexes, one not based on confrontation, competition or sexual demands. Men and women can learn to develop qualities previously hidden away under fear and habits.

Active audience
Contact performances normally take place in studios, art galleries or public places. The onlookers sit close to the performers who try, rather than be dazzlingly impressive, to get the spectators to become part in the event itself, avoiding the typical producer/consumer relationship. A typical reaction after contact improvisation performances was a spontaneous joining in by the audience. Seemingly the body had been awakened, the kinaesthetic sense stimulated, expressed through activity. Instead of

leaning back and expecting something to be done for them as when watching television, the audience feel and perceives things happening in their own bodies.

Informality was one of the basic premises. The dancers felt that in order to make a performance, no stage, no lighting, not even an audience was needed! If a person is dancing with an undivided attention on the "now", the present happenings, they are, in a way, independent of the audience. On the other hand, they can share this event with those present and make it into a joint experience. This takes place under the motto," we are engaged in something, find ourselves in a creative process. If you want to come along and take part, great! If not, that's fine as well!"

Everyone is an artist and dancer!
Western civilisation tends to couple artistic expression with accomplishment and productivity. Especially with dance, the criteria for beauty and worth are technical perfection and virtuosity. But in order for us to express ourselves we don't need to be the "perfect" dancer, on the contrary - it is about the joy of dancing.

B CONTACT IMPROVISATION STRUCTURE

1 IMPROVISATION – THE DYNAMIC OF THE PROVISIONAL

"Improvisation, in my way of handling, demands a constant connection with some thing – object, action and/ or mood in a situation. (...) One must take a chance on the fitness of one's own instincts. (...) In the improvisation, at the moment of moving into an action; one must behave and feel as though no other choice exists ... "[26]

Yvonne Rainer

Improvisation can be defined as creating an event without prior agreement or planning. The material for this event is only limited by its availability. As long as something is being improvised it is inherently non-hierarchical, for true improvisation the mind must remain open. We cannot act as if we already know the answers to the questions or the directions in which the situation leads us. We need to trust that the moment, a movement, a direction, an impulse - will lead to something new. Improvisation is also about letting go - if a jump, a movement sequence, an acrobatic *"trick"* didn't work, stop trying: it is simply the wrong moment.

Discipline within contact improvisation is to be and remain in the present with your partner - NOW ! *Improvisation is the art of the immediate.* Finely tuned to your present state, that of your partner, your environment, the atmosphere, the dynamic of continual change and awareness of what is, not what you think it should be!

Through improvisation we can learn to trust the process, learn to let go of concepts and to perceive the endless possibilities available in the moment.

Trust is deference to what is happening. On the other hand, if something is inappropriate, use this momentary impulse to change it. The questions arising out of one person jumping, the other rolling, are considerable - where can these to actions meet? How are decisions made? Who is leading? Why? How?

Successful improvisation produces unique transient choreographies, as Pauline de Groot explains: *"Improvisation: the challenge to make decisions in the nick of time, or to risk postponing decisions and spend time in an open moment, in undecided time, to walk the unclaimed/ uncultivated terrain between activities, so that decision makes itself, is not wrought up but is guided by an alertness to the forces and emotions at play at the moment - the intensity of light, sound and movement, and their placement and displacement in space. In this play of forces, a state of mind, an atmosphere and temperature is generated between performer and watcher. This can never be reclaimed - in any case, not with the impact and sharpness of the moment. the challenge is in generating this fullness, not in claiming its final form."[27]*

Photo 8:
Karen Nelson and Andrew
Harwood, 1986
(Photo: Bill Arnold)

25 Questions on Improvisation

gathered from teachers and students during the Summer Dance Course "On Improvisation," June 1985 at the Theaterschool Modern Dance Department, Amsterdam, Netherlands.

1. Is improvisation one thing or is it many different things?
2. Imagination and structure, where are we free?
3. How does imagination relate to form?
4. Is improvisation in dance only the lack of set material?
5. How can you use feedback (video, audio, discussion) in working with improvisation?
6. Is improvisation a technique?
7. Do animals improvise?
8. How do you develop skill in improvisation?
9. How does improvisation apply to physical training? To body work? to technique?
10. How does the activity of research relate to the performance situation or can we continue the sensibility of research in performance?
11. What does limitation, structure and rule do to improvisation?
12. What do we want the audience to know about improvisation?
13. How do you relate to the audience while improvising?
14. Creative process and improvisation. The same thing?
15. What are the perceptual skills of improvisation?
16. What are the criteria for evaluating improvisation?
17. Can the same standards be used to evaluate the success of an improvised performance as are used to evaluate a performance of set movement?
18. Is improvisation a political choice?
19. Are there specific skills, either physical or creative, that facilitate the learning of improvisation?
20. What do you do as a teacher of improvisation, if your students understand the assignment in a way it is not meant?
21. How can there be such a difference between the experience of doing an improvisation and the seeing of an improvisation from the outside?
22. Is improvisation anarchism?
23. What is the relation between improvising and life?
24. Is a cathedral built over a period of 200 years on improvisation?
25. How do you know the ending of an improvisation?

Improvisation and hierarchy are as noted above, connected themes. A tradition in contact improvisation is that the teacher does provide many explanations. They offer a problem and say, " find a solution but I'm not going to show you mine!" it is a guidance to a particular area which can be explored. If suggestions do arise, they should be seen as a part of a vocabulary not as part of the alphabet.

1.1 Dancing duets

"A duet is composition for two voices, instruments, or bodies. It is a relationship in which two people share. It is a partnership. (...) One responds to the other, a dialogue or conversation occurs in the interaction."[28]

Adwoa Lemieux

Contact improvisation is usually done with a partner though within free improvisation and jams, trios and other constellations can form. The duet-dance has rules differing from other dance forms: the shared dance, the dialogue lives in continual giving-of-weight through a mutual contact point. From this, something unique is created and you often find yourself in a unexpected position or emotional state.

Photo 9:
Thomas Kaltenbrunner and Brigitte Zeeh in "Hommage au coeur", 1995

1.2 Contact and contact points

"Two bodies move in permanent contact with each other... the movement is guided by the ability of the dancers to keep this constant contact and to give each other physical support...."[29]

Cynthia J. Novack

The human body allows communication and exchange through the various external and internal surfaces (skin, lungs, intestinal tract for instance). The central role within contact improvisation is played by the coming together of two surfaces, the point of contact. All movement in the dance stems from this point and leads to a spontaneous physical dialogue, provided that both participators stay open and receptive for each other.

To come into contact with someone is the prerequisite for receiving information and communication. In contact improvisation it is important to be deeply aware of one's own momentary state and to be centred before coming into "contact" with someone else.

Photo 10

43

1.3 Giving and taking of weight _____

"In Contact Improvisation, the functional use of touching predominates. The form depends on communication between dancers through the sense of touch and weight."[30]

Cynthia J. Novack

The point of contact is maintained through a continual giving of weight. The roles of giver and taker are continually switching. When we give weight, we are also, in some way, forced into surrendering control, letting go of the need to hold on but without collapsing. An frequently used image for this process is - giving weight is like pouring fine sand into a bucket.

The taking of weight means most of all, a solid support for your partner but without overtaxing yourself. Trying to take too much weight can be dangerous and lead to injury. It is about *"along the easiest pathways available to the mutual moving mass."*[31] *(Steve Paxton)*.

We can also talk about the giving and taking of emotional weight. Before we can give, we have to sense a readiness, a support ,both physical and emotional, from our partner. In contact improvisation, this creation of emotional and physical trust in our partner often leads to situations and positions which, having been pre- viously unexplored, create anxiety and fear.

Photo 11

44

1.4 Movement flow

"Birthing my baby boy was the essence of a contact dance. For me, the key to a satisfying improvisational dance means abandoning my analytical mind and embracing the center of my intuitive self. .... I danced my baby out into this world, and he danced with me. Now, when we hold each other and move together through our days and nights I feel the continuation of our original improv on the day he was born"[32]

Lisa Gottlieb-Clark

We have seen that the actual process of coming into contact needs an intimacy and readiness to be open to a partner - just these first few steps can be extremely intensive. A contact-dancer attunes themselves to their partner, responds, and receives continual physical feedback from the mass, momentum and touch of the partner - literally a sensitive relationship!

With the aim of finding the paths of least resistance, the economy of the moment, the dance produces a steadily flowing unit. Many technical exercises in contact improvisation lead to a deeper understanding of the basic principle - the energy pathway. This may sound rather intellectually vague but as Curt Siddall explains: *"is more clearly understood when experienced. However it may be thought of as the path of least resistance in the moment to moment reality of each dancer."[33]* When two dancers have found this energy pathway, this mutual movement flow, many decisions are resolved by the situation itself: the dancers experience a time of simultaneous activity and passivity.

Photo 12: (Photo: Tom Erikson)

45

C THE BASICS OF MOVEMENT

The human body, as every "body" in the universe, is governed by the laws of nature. It is a active, biological body with its own unique bio-mechanism. The vital energy of the neuro-muscular system is in an incessant conflict with these laws. For instance, standing upright in spite of gravity, through the supportive structures of the skeleton (see Release Technique). Contact improvisation investigates and uses these laws - a thorough knowledge of the connection between gravity and momentum for instance is important for the dancer as a whole. Apart from the physical and biological aspects of our body, we also have to consider the emotional, the spiritual sides which enable us to communicate and create. Without this consideration, contact improvisation would be deprived of its "heart". It is important therefore that we take the following few chapters about the physical and biological body "to heart".

1 THE PHYSICAL BODY IN SPACE AND TIME: WEIGHT, GRAVITY AND MOMENTUM

"Every weight desires to descend to the centre by the shortest way; and where there is the greater weight, there is the greater desire."[34]

Leonardo da Vinci

1.1. Bio-mechanical fundamentals

1.1.1 What is weight ?

This chapter explores the "solid" body in its physical environment. In physics, the intrinsic property of all matter and energy and the source of gravitational field is defined as mass. It is perceived as an object's weight or its inertia (its reluctance to change its motion). Weight however, is defined as the downward-acting force on an object due to gravitational attraction.

To give weight, onto the back of your partner for instance, means therefore the giving of mass, gravitationally connected through your partner to the centre of the earth.

We don't have to give the whole of our mass, we can lean against someone as well if we meet an equal opposing force. This is *Newton's* third law: Every action has an opposite and equal reaction.

In contact improvisation we can see this when one partner offers their weight to the other. If there is no resistance to that force, both dancers end up sliding to the floor.

The taking of weight means the "taker" maintains enough force to give resistance to the "giver". This maintenance of force can be made by using ones own physical weight, structural force (the skeleton) or muscular force. There are often situations however where it is not clearly defined who is the giver and who is the taker. This is an important principle in contact improvisation, ensuring the liveliness of the dance. The learning process involves finding out how to use just the right amount of force needed to support.

1.1.2 Centre of gravity

All the physical forces which affect our bodies are united in the centre of gravity. A line drawn from this point towards the middle of the earth is called the gravitational axis. In a normal extended position, the centre of gravity is near the centre of the body. (see photo 13).

Photo 13: Heike Wrede in "Frei Schwimmen", 1996. (Photo: Tom Erikson)

The exact position of the centre of gravity depends of course on stature, body type, alignment and spatial positioning. If we bend forward for instance, the centre of gravity lies outside of our body.

Stable and precarious balance.
Using the example from above of leaning forward, we can see that there are different forms of balance. When standing, the centre of gravity is found to be directly above the supporting surfaces (the feet). If we lean forward slightly, the centre of gravity shifts in the same direction and up to a certain point, a return to centre is possible. This could be called a precarious balance. If this point is exceeded and the centre of gravity lies outside of our body, we fall down. We can also define the centre of gravity as a point where a body is perfectly balanced. If we could be continually supported at this point, we could turn and revolve in all directions and never be out of balance. For contact improvisation this means whenever the centre of gravity is not above the point of contact, the body will tend to fall towards wherever the centre of gravity finds itself at that moment.

Whatever happens during the dance, it always follows the natural laws. Often we experience less of a sense of where the centre is than the consequences of this centre shifting.

Photo 14

A shared centre of gravity .
During contact improvisation duets we often find ourselves in situations where both bodies can be defined as one unit. There is a common centre of gravity, a shared gravitational axis (see photo 14). Its exact position is dependent on the amount of shared weight and the position of the individual centres. Through two precarious balances a stable unity is created.

1.2 Using gravity to move

In our bodies is a constant interplay between gravity and movement. When we move, the action happens through two physical alignments - one with gravity and one against. If we lift our arm to shoulder height for example, and then let go, the arm falls towards the gravitational source. We can use the following definitions to illustrate the point:

1. **Gravity:** gravity is a natural force, a constant pull on all bodies towards the (earth's) centre.

2. **Inertia:** the reluctance of a massive object to change its motion. Inertia is inherent to mass, present even in the absence of gravity. We can sense inertia in dance, when we try to change direction. The previous direction still exerts a conservative force onto the new movement. We find similarities when resting on the floor. Isn't it often hard work trying to come from the floor to standing?

3. **Momentum:** defined as the product of mass and velocity. Using the example of the lifted arm: the higher the arm, the quicker the fall therefore more momentum.

Photo 15: (Photo: Archiv Scott Wells)

In contact improvisation, the centre of gravity is shifted on purpose in order to move. When rolling over your partner, posture is altered, changing the centre of gravity and support point and through this, movement originates. It does not occur through a intentional pushing or pulling but solely through the displacement of the (common) centre of gravity. Gravity does the rest, giving an impulse for the next movement. The shared movement with a partner can be seen as coming from this alteration of the centre of gravity, caused by either or both of the dancers (see photo 15). It could be that the physical and emotional buoyancy created by doing or watching contact improvisation comes from the support and movement created within the non-invasive, informal and aggression-free atmosphere.

1.3 Bio-mechanics of lifting, jumping and spiralling

Balance and stability depends on, as mentioned above, the relation between the gravitational axis and the supporting surfaces. The height of the centre of gravity is also important.

1. *Lifting:* we can sense this relationship between two centres of gravity when we lift a heavy object. Much less force or effort is needed when the object is close to our centre. In other words two points of balance become one!

There are several locations on our body which are particularly useful when it comes to lifting: the thigh, sacrum ,shoulders. If we support and lift someone using the lower part of the spine, the individual centres of gravity concur, resulting in an relatively effortless means of carrying. Another interesting phenomenon can be observed here as well: if the one being carried relaxes all muscle tone and acts like a sack of potatoes, the carrier will sense it as being unbearably heavy. If, one the other hand, the one on top stretches and tones the muscle, it becomes much easier to lift and balance.

*Photo 16: Scott Wells & Samantha Beers
(Photo: David Papas)*

2. *Jumping:* the easiest way of catching a leaping partner is to position your own centre of gravity under the highest point of the jump. Here, the jump has ceased to be a jump and has not yet become a fall, and collision can be avoided. The resulting momentum leads easily into shared movement in space. It is helpful to imagine jumping into your partner's centre of gravity rather than against it.

3. *Spiralling:* sharply defined, angular movement needs a lot of energy to stop, change direction and accelerate again. In contrast, circular, round or spirallic movement is in effect a permanent change of direction and is

51

therefore much easier to vary and alter. If the spirallic form is central to the dance, flowing, smooth movement results - a continual exploitation of momentum.

Weight becomes movement.

Gravity gives impetus for movement: the characteristic movement principles in contact improvisation originate through the various factors described above. As soon as contact to the supporting surface is lost, the individual (and shared) centre of gravity disappears, and we become a precarious victim of gravity. From this instant of falling /letting go, the body has the chance to use the generated momentum to find new directions, new movement. This use of momentum enables muscular energy to be reduce to a minimum and central to contact improvisation, movement is created by gravitational forces on mass, aka weight!

When a body moves though, the physics gets complicated! Momentum, acceleration, angular velocity, inertia etc all have to be considered.

Many points of contact.

In contact improvisation, weight is shared or shifted through the point of contact. There are however, moments when more contact points or surfaces occur; when leaning against a wall for instance. Apart from Gravity and the floors " reaction", all other forces have to be considered.

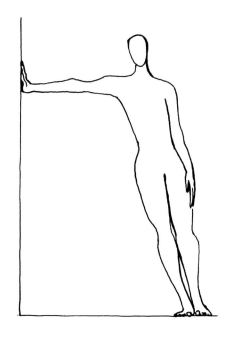

Figure 3

Summary

Gravity, inertia and momentum are forces occurring in every movement. An physical investigation into these forces can lead to more agility, joy and fun when dancing. Movements become energised when we let go of our dominating intellect and allow the natural forces to take over (again). Walking becomes easier if we lean forward a little and let Gravity, inertia and momentum take their effect. Maybe the fascination of swings and roundabouts in children comes from an exciting sense of harmony with your body and these fundamental forces. Likewise, when parents rock their children in their arms: feelings of protection and calm arise when gravity, inertia, momentum and resistance (the parent's hands) are physically experienced...

Contact improvisation is not just an abstract form though. It is not just concerned with the physics of movement but the human aspect of these forces. It is about communication and sharing. One element which we can experience jointly : playing with the consequences of these physical powers.

Photo 17:
Lisa Schmidt and Dieter Heitkamp in "Augenblick-licht"
(Photo: Sebastian Greuner)

Photo 18: Kurt Koegel, Ka Rustler, Dieter Heitkamp (Photo: Udo Hesse)

54

2 THE BIOLOGICAL BODY: FLEXIBLE, LIVELY AND INTELLIGENT

"Out of the warm, pulsating, lively body, her imagination made a ghost. Her self manipulated a dead thing.... how do you see your body at the moment?"[35]

Peter Schellenbaum

This chapter, in contrast to the last chapter's investigation of the *cold*, physical body, will look at the flexible, vital, anatomical personal body.

Movement is often made using much too much muscular tension. Dance appears stiff, the body seems to be made up of isolated parts and when dancing together, the dancers get tangled up and blocked. If we learn to relax the relevant musculature, loosening up in the joints, natural, harmonious and organic movement can take place. To relax does not mean to collapse or simply to get comfortable. Relaxing is finding the delicate balance between a relaxed tension and a tense relaxation.

A stable posture come from a good alignment of the skeleton, especially the spinal column (see the section on Release Technique). The weight bearing system is not the musculature but the skeleton. The vertical system of bones directs the weight downwards with the resistance of the floor replying with an upward supportive force. This give and take enables an economic use of force in contact improvisation.

It is also helpful to consider the spiral as a form of movement at this point: turning around and within each other, using the spiral to stand and to fall, makes use of momentum and promotes a smooth flow of movement.

Relaxation and support from the skeleton increases the load- bearing capacity of many bodily surfaces during contact improvisation; the sacrum, shoulders and thighs for example.

2.1 The intelligent body ——————————————

The human body has its own *autonomous intelligence* when it comes to movement. It reacts independently, has instinctive reflexes and functions most effectively therefore with minimum interference from "will -power".

In contact improvisation, we talk about the "responsive body", a body capable of autonomous decision making and instinctive reaction (*responsibility = response ability*). Trust in this ability of the body plays an especially large role when falling: we can either fall smoothly and trustingly melt into the supporting surfaces or produce a fearful collision.

This "responsive body" is not just a bundle of nervous reflexes, becoming active only in times of emergency, but a way of (human) being, in harmony with the natural laws of the physical surroundings. Ideally the "responsive body" stands for something primeval, real and spiritual in contrast to self-indulgence and egotistic confrontation.

2.2 Movement possibilities in space and time ─────

Every movement of a living body takes place in space, needs time, has a definite form and uses a certain amount of force. An awareness of these factors can lead to an increase in sensitivity to one's own movement patterns. This awareness will also help to find new possibilities within a pre-determined movement structure.

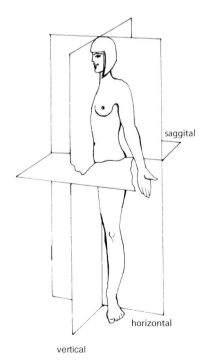

Figure 4: Planes

a) Orientation in space
   1. Spatial areas : high, medium, deep
   2. Bodily dimensions : vertical, horizontal, sagittal
   3. Directional change : up/down, left/right, forwards, backwards

b) The Kinesphere- the personal body zone.
   Each person has their own unique sphere of space around them in which they move. This is called the kinesphere. It can be separated into three parts:
   - The close kinesphere is the area in the immediate vicinity of the body. (the area used when we write, for instance).
   - the medium kinesphere, from bent elbows to the fingertips. This is the area used for communication in our culture.
   - the large kinesphere is the area reached by outstretched arms and legs.

c) General movement possibilities
   1. Formation of physical actions : walking, shift of weight, jumping, turning, gesticulating.
   2. Articulation of body parts: bending, stretching, turning, abduction and adduction (away from and towards the axis).
   3. Initiation - where does the movement come from?
   4. Body and body parts: the unity of the body parts, posture, gesture, simultaneous or sequential use.

3 THE MINDFUL BODY: SELF-AWARENESS, TOUCH AND COMMUNICATION

3.1 Self-awareness is body-awareness

" our bodies and minds are not two and not one...
our bodies and minds are both two and one"[36]

Suzuki Roshi

We normally differentiate between mind and body and endorse this dualism of a mindless body and disembodied soul. But when we meet someone, we do not encounter an animate corpse behind which presumably, is the soul. We are always confronted with a vital being with their own individual "gestalt". *Graf Dürckheim,* a German authority in eastern philosophy, says that we do not just have the body but we are a body (he uses the word *"Leib"* from which comes the English word - life.)

"... the living body is always an active body. Human movement though, is more than just a physical operation. It is a permanent expression of life of the whole person and what is affecting (moving) them at that specific instance. So seen, movement is an active gesture and the body (Leib) is not solely a vessel to be perceived, observed, examined and repaired by our unattached minds and souls. The body is the person, in the form of a gestural unity, expressing and presenting its self to the world."[37]

Dürckheim distinguished three different levels of existence for this *"Leib".* The first is responsible for health and optimal functioning which is a prerequisite for further development. the second level is more aesthetically orientated and the third ultimately has its concern with a personal "inner transcendence".

Movement is here more than bio-mechanics, it is the holistic expression of a person and what "moves" them. Maybe it is not by chance that we say we have had a "moving experience".

58

3.2 Touch

"I value this work not only for the rare glimpses of in-touch, in-time, in-tune, but for the companionship of the ever present indications of what is possible. The form itself, if one exists beyond the instances of attempts to experience it, is none other than the existence of the possibility of a dance in which wills, instincts and verges merge. Emergency, emerge, merge. It amounts to having to believe in a possibility which one may never have experienced."[38]

Christina Svane

A lot of communication can function over a relatively large distance, but touch is the personal language of intimacy and so being, one of the most potent channels for communication : touch overcomes isolation, too little creates isolation. Touch, to be touched can have many different qualities: supportive, calming, tenderness, sexual, aggressive, playful, exciting - depending on the intention and state of the people involved.

The decision to dance contact improvisation is at the same time a decision for touch. The giving and taking of weight in order to move with a partner cannot take place without it! Through this contact point, the touching surfaces, comes a mind-body dialogue of movement. Contact improvisation does not insist on a constant physical contact with your partner: it is also possible to continue this relationship and communication when spatially separated.

Touch sensitises, promotes awareness and is one of the most important means of communication in contact improvisation - to perceive your own and your partners physical limits, discover mutual support, the creation of trust. Feelings and sensuality are other connected aspects. Thus touch is a touching experience!

3.3 Trust

"it's important that students notice .... the trust and confidence they gain in themselves and their partners to stay with a moment, and meet the needs of each changing moment....Trust, patiently nurtured through confidence and familiarity, prepares the way for diversity. Through trust, awkward, uncomfortable moments of vulnerability and powerful moments of virtuosity become equally rich."[39]

Randy Warshaw

Touch and a sense of ease can only exist within an atmosphere of trust. It is important therefore, to respect the need for physical and emotional security from the beginning. Emotional support can be communicated through physical contact as well as a positive approach to your partner through eye-contact, attentiveness and interest.

Each person has a sense of how far or how near they can be approached without their personal space being invaded (see: kinesphere). It is important in contact improvisation to have absolute respect for this space and a clear awareness of where these edges are but as *Nancy Stark Smith* writes: "..*it seems the edges are moveable - that by sensing the limit, respecting it, you encourage it to open. A push comes to a shove. But if you go only as far as you are welcome ,you are invited back.*"[40] Through a willingness to dance contact improvisation, you are allowing each other to approach this personal space, get close to the edge - but it is not an invitation for invasion!

Contact improvisation can help towards a self-discernment, a giving of weight/self without squashing, giving support, taking physical and emotional risks, abandoning restraint, spontaneity - in other words : overcoming feelings of isolation through touch and movement.

Touch can release underlying feelings which are not consciously accessible. Contact improvisation however, should not be seen as a therapy. This aspect is of course recognised and is accepted into the movement process for emotions have their own flow and are in constant change. As *Karen Nelson* puts it: "*Contact is a Touch Revolution, it's a revolution against the tyranny of non-touch. It's a politic of movement from the inside out, organizing to break the code of space and distance between people. We know of a lover's touch, or family and friends touch, but the touch of a virtual stranger is left to chance brushes in crowded places, like the palm of my hand where the fingertips of the cashier delivers change for my dollar.*"[41]

Photo 19

3.4 Sensuality and sexuality

"Touch and sex lie in close proximity. But they are not alone. Touch, along with the other senses, integrates our physicality. In this way, it relates to everything.... Sex is in there, someplace, everyplace. It is difficult to imagine that while grazing each other's minds in touch and movement we would not bump into some of its manifestations."[42]

Steve Paxton

It is often not easy to sanction physical closeness. It is important to first respect the physical borders of each other and not make excessive demands. With each new dance and new partner, a new consensus must be reached.

All surfaces and areas of the body are used as shared surfaces in contact improvisation. This also includes areas of the body usually considered as taboo. The need for close physical contact and sexuality are often confused in our society and can lead to confusion. Agreements are made between the dancers in contact improvisation: personal/private borders are to be respected and made clearly evident. Whatever happens during a contact dance has no further social consequences afterwards. There is a difference between allowing emotions to occur and acting upon them, whether sexual or hostile. Contact improvisation offers an open and secure framework to look at these feelings, without succumbing to them, something which outside of contact improvisation, normally happens.

This mutual dance promotes a playful dexterity with these aspects and a way of *"flexing and stretching comfort zones".* Sympathy, antipathy, eroticism or aggression flow together in the shared experience of dance and give it new vitality and intensity.

As mentioned before, at the beginning of contact improvisation, emotions, sensuality and sex were omitted as areas of inquiry, in order to concentrate purely on the physicality of the dance. But nowadays, a growing interest in these other themes can be observed. A few issues of Contact Quarterly have been entirely concerned with sexuality and identity (Vol.21 No.1 & 2) and there were special workshops - "School of Sensitivity - Contact & Sexuality" led by *Dieter Heitkamp* in Berlin - was one. He wrote : *"Life is sensational. And so is dancing. Combining sexual and heart energy. The four directions of the heart: Unprejudice (Unvoreingenommenheit), Compassion, Affection, Love. Red, bloodful, wild, beefy dancing. There is risk-taking involved, but also care. Caring for oneself, a partner, a group."*[43]

3.5 Communication _____

"Contact improvisation is concerned with intuition, aesthetics, physicality, being in the moment .... it is a communications network which provides a framework for the dancers. The focus is on the here-and-now of communication and how with every dance, it is created anew". [44]

Keriac

All previously addressed aspects of human existence are not isolated entities, but are embedded in a larger whole: the physical body in a time-space construction of elementary forces of nature; the biological body in a finely poised balance with its ecosystem (breathing, eating, defecation); the mindful body in a social structure.

The common denominators in all of these systems are communication and exchange. These systems are of course concurrent with each other. The separation of body, mind and soul into physical, biological and spiritual divisions is an artificial one and is only useful when looking for a deeper understanding of each area. In contact improvisation all sides are involved in a free transaction (improvisation) and come together in a mutual, personal "meeting through movement" (contact). The contact-duets can therefore be described as a mirror for interpersonal relationships and communication.

Photo 20

II PRACTICE

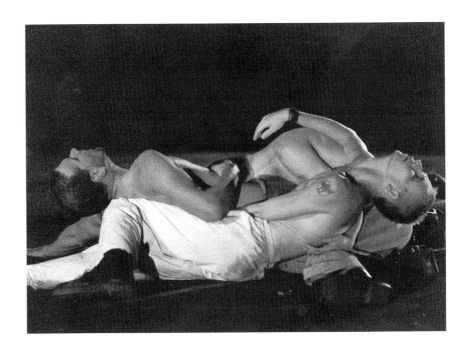

Photo 21: Antagon Theater in „Schreie Niemandsland", 1996
(Photo: Susanne Lindner)

A LEARNING CONTACT IMPROVISATION: INQUISITIVENESS AND SELF-DISCOVERY

1 CONTACT AND IMPROVISATION : SENSITIVITY AND AWARENESS SKILLS, PERCEPTUAL STATES AND PHYSICAL SKILLS

"The dancing does the teaching: The teacher points to that."[45]

Steve Paxton

In order to keep a structure to the subject matter dealt with in this section, three aspects of Contact and Improvisation have been defined:
1. Sensitivity and Awareness Skills
2. Perceptual states
3. Physical skills

1.1 Sensitivity and Awareness skills

"When dealing with sensitive areas of any sort, we should dance sensitively and, as in other civilized discourse, if discord arises, change the subject or watch our steps."[46]

Steve Paxton

To be aware of your own body is a natural prerequisite for dance and improvisation. This awareness is strongly bound to the kinaesthetic sense. This is really a bundle of five different senses : temperature perception, tactile sense (pressure, touch, pain), spatial orientation and balance. All this information about the state of our body is transformed into a holistic movement-sense. On top of this, information is added from our lungs, muscle-tone, rate of pulse etc. *Steve Paxton* often provides simple exercises towards an unaffected perception of what we are seeing, smelling, hearing, feeling. It is about getting away from the rational world of concepts towards the actual world of perception and from this starting point, beginning to dance. Basically, this is all there is to be "done". *Paxton* began in the eighties to work with blind people because of their compensatory enhancement of the other senses due to lack of sight.

1.1.1 Body surfaces and sensitising the skin

".....the skin works most of the time on automatic pilot. The conscious mind is alerted if unusual stimulation appears on the surface of the body, but I don't notice the touch of my clothes or my weight in a chair most of the time.... and relying on [the skin's] information to protect me, to warn me, to feed back to me the data to which I am responding."[47]

Steve Paxton

Being aware of the body surfaces is important for the perception of inside/outside, your own physical "edges" and it's encounter with other bodies. Normally though, most of these sensations pass us by - the weight and texture of our clothing is seldom perceived. Dancing however, is a sensual, osmotic experience and total sensory awareness is essential. The skin, the largest of our sensory organs, has a complete directional awareness and in contact improvisation, is the eye with which we see, the surface through which weight is transferred. The skin is also the one of the most important sensory organs responsible for our feelings of well-being and delight.

1.1.2 Mental and physical relaxation

"Trusting now this process as other times I trusted the standing and the crawling, the wandering in the room ... the shifting and the lolling twisting on the floor ... the rolling over and trusting to the enjoying that would lead to some finding ... "[48]

Simone Forti

It is very difficult to be free flowing and playful when dancing if our body is blocked up tight and our thoughts are holding on tight to their pre-conceived ideas. A lot of time is spent coming to states of both mental and physical ease in contact improvisation. Ease also means giving up the need to understand, to relinquish intellectual control of the situation and the resulting movements. In order to relax "into" the dancing, our awareness is guided towards the point of contact, the movement flow, the environment or the resulting movement material. Relaxing does not mean to collapse or passivity though!

66

1.2 Perceptual states_____

"Its a lot like when children play. Being familar with the experiences we had when we were younger, that kind of curiosity in making contact with the environment – taste everything, hear everything, make noise, see if you could hurt it, see if it could hurt you – that interaction (...) that's a kind of a magical state of play."[49]

Lisa Nelson

A *state* can be described as a mental condition, a mood, ambience; a plane of consciousness into which one can be led. There are different qualities of perception, different levels of experience in which we can find ourselves - the "now" of the body-mind-spirit being. *States* can have many forms - absolute concentration and total focus of energy for instance. Various exercises take on a priming function for these states, for example dancing blindfold over an extended period of time or protracted repetition of a dynamic movement phrase. There are also exercises which can be done within a group: getting used to the floor through sitting to standing, walking, running and falling once more to the floor, to sitting to standing .....

One clear demarcation between *Skills* and *States* came about during an annual Contact Teachers Conference. The starting point was the question: how can I create conditions which nurture curiosity and learning?"

Various states were discussed, relating to physical, emotional, rhythmic, ecstatic, space/time or archetypal aspects. Sensual, erotic/sexual and spiritual states were also talked about which, under specific conditions, we can attain. A unifying system for these *states* was not found. Certain perceptions, feelings or the diverse attributes of attentiveness and presence lead to clearly disparate experiences but are as such, very difficult to verbalise. A *state* is one way to enter a dance.

Research into the multitudinous forms of experience is important because, as *Keriac* states: "each form these states take influences the outcome of the dance". When we start a dance from the focus of a specific state, the awareness is directed towards a particular area and results in a very different dance than without this explicit attention. This experimentation with states in order to get new insights of ones self is a very different style of teaching than found in a ballet class!

1.2.1 Mindfulness and peripheral awareness

"Interest is simply applying awareness to what goes on in your everyday life. Awareness while you are cooking, awareness while you are driving, awareness while you are changing diapers, even awareness while you are arguing. Such awareness can help to free you from speed, chaos, neurosis, and resentment of all kinds. It can free you from the obstacles to nowness, so that you can cheer up on the spot, all the time."[50]

Chögyam Trungpa

In order to find an awareness of this deeper self, It is necessary to develop skills in focusing and maintaining sensory attention onto something definite. Two aspects can be illustrative:

a) Mindfulness
Mindfulness is the ability to fix the attention / mind onto a point or activity - a movement phrase while dancing for instance.

Our mind is usually unsettled, leaping from one thought to another - emotions are similarly transitory. Likewise, our inner-awareness is usually scattered around, seldom is it focussed in the here-and-now. But if the body and mind do not work in sync, the mind absents itself from a dis-integrating body. Mindfulness when dancing means a precise awareness of the movement activity, a sense of the floor under your feet, being alert to every minute change in physical and mental attitudes. This can be viewed as "experiencing the moment".

Harmonising mind and body in this way encourages us to get away from a visual and literal interpretation of the world - we often get involved with an incessant inner dialogue of words and pictures which is mostly no more than subconscious blabber and private daydreams. We involve our selves in conflict and argument - primarily in our own heads! What happens if we stop doing this for a while?

Shambala wrote: "If you are able to relax – relax to a cloud by looking at it, relax to a drop of rain and experience its genueness – you can see the unconditionality of reality, which remains very simply in things as they are , very simply."[51]

68

Photo 22: Thomas Kaltenbrunner in "Step out – perky!", 1995
(Photo: Tom Erikson)

b) Spatial awareness and peripheral vision.
Spatial awareness is the ability to address attention towards the immediate surroundings: The space surrounding the body while dancing for example.

A key principle in contact improvisation draws on this concept - a defocussing of the eyes. We are not fixed on any particular point in space but try to take in everything around us. This peripheral vision provides us with impartial information from the total field of vision (normally almost 180 degrees). This extended spatial awareness is especially necessary when dancing within groups - it helps to prevent collisions with other duets and consequently furthers the essential freedom and openness needed during contact.

The first requirement is a *mindfulness*, a focussed awareness onto what is happening now - moment by moment. From this state, a comprehensive "gaze" into the surrounding space can develop. Without this attention for yourself and the immediate surroundings, the danger exists of losing yourself and "spacing out"!

Mindfulness and peripheral awareness are not as such mental processes but rather an openness to the existing situation, which can be compared to some forms of meditation. We can perhaps get a feeling for this state if we do the following exercise:

While you are reading this sentence - keep looking at the page and not moving your eyes, take your awareness towards the outermost point of your vision on the left , then back towards the middle and then to the right extreme. What kinds of things did you discern? what do you perceive at the upper and lower extremes of your field of vision? What do you sense of the world behind you? Noises? Impressions? Stay in this process for a while and then return to "normality". Has anything in the way of your contact with the world changed?

1.3 Physical skills ———————————————————————————

"It does take some physical skill and listening ability to communicate timing, impulse and subtlety of moving weight and support (...) To engage the senses, gross and subtle, is an overwhelming field of discovery."[52]

Karen Nelson

There are of course many different physical skills which help us to be at ease with dancing and extend our range of movement vocabulary. The point of learning these skills is not a development of perfect technique and acrobatic accomplishment but rather a personal broadening of expressive potential. Basically it is about enriching the dance. Apart from this, it also increases the fun had while dancing and makes it a lot less dangerous when flexibility, reflex, and movement are attuned. Physical skills means primarily, achieving a sense of the body surfaces, making it "round" and "soft", and being able to find a continuous flow of movement.

Important skills are:

- experiencing mass/weight.
- playing with and moving this mass.
- sensing the point of contact.
- rolling, turning, falling.
- a gradual transference of weight.
- learning to support.

2 WARMING UP

"An important objective of warming up is to bring the attention into the physical body - away from mental control and a targeted "use".[53]

Keriac

In contact improvisation, a lot of time is spent in relaxing and in gentle warm-ups, in order to achieve a preparedness of body and mind for the approaching dance.

A physically appropriate warm-up is necessary to:
- arrive in the space - or to "land".
- develop a sense of timing.
- orient oneself in the space.
- stretch the "kinesphere".
- get accustomed to your partner
- broaden the peripheral field of vision

it often starts with a personal warm-up - for instance 10 minutes of doing what each person needs to do in order to "land", running, walking, stretching, whatever is necessary to get to the here-and-now. It often happens with experienced groups, that a collective "spirit" is achieved despite each person warming up alone.

2.1 Warming up ideas

The following ideas come from general warming-up methods as well as more specific contact improvisation and New Dance exercises. They include themes such as relaxation, increasing awareness, stretching etc. Because contact improvisation is always improvised, you should play with these exercises and not feel bound. What is most important: not all of these exercises are suitable for everybody, each person should be encouraged to sense what they need and to do just that, not be forced into doing something else.

2.1.1 General warming up

Before it starts : "arrive" and get a sense of the floor.
1. Lie with your back on the floor
2. What does the floor feel like? Be aware of temperature, hardness, softness...

3. Imagine that you are becoming softer and softer, giving up more and more weight into the floor.
4. Rock slowly from left to right. This should happen through a gentle shifting of weight, not a wilful force. Keep increasing the rocking until you turn over and come to rest on your belly.
5. Enjoy this moment of ease then commence rolling again and travel around the room.
6. It doesn't matter if you meet another person on your journey. Roll carefully around or over this person.

a) moving in space
Orang-utan
1. Let your upper body hang loosely towards the floor.
2. Move around the room like an ape, let your hands take a little weight
3. Roll forward from your feet and repeat this movement with your hands.
4. Place weight onto your hands, roll gently with your feet, lift them up and bring them in front of your hands like an Orang-utan. Move around the space.

Further suggestions:
- give a bit more weight into the hands
- try an occasional hand-stand
- without using momentum from your feet, try to get your hips up against the wall.

Pushing
1. Lie on the floor next to a partner. Let your feet touch your partners feet. Now push them away.
2. Push yourself away from a wall, the floor, a partner.

Invent your own T'ai Chi
(It is not necessary to have knowledge of T'ai Chi to do this exercise. Make your own!)
1. T'ai chi: make flowing movements with your arms and legs and hips. Discover your own style.
2. Karate : kick your feet out in all different directions, with each kick, shout " Ki-ai" or "Hah".

Jumping like a frog.
1. Crouch down like a frog.
2. Collect your energy and with a loud shout, explode into a forward "frog" jump, leaving your feet in place.
Further suggestions: Crouch down facing a partner, making sure you have enough distance between you. Repeat the frog jump towards your partner, keep in eye contact!

Photo 23

b) Mobilising the joints.
Isolation exercises
1. Stand loose and relaxed, your feet parallel and directly below the hip sockets.
2. Turn and twist first the feet, then knees, left/right thigh, pelvis, shoulders, left/right arm, wrists, fingers etc. move each body part in isolation.
3. Afterwards move, for example, your left knee and right shoulder together. Play with different combinations. See if you can move all your joints at the same time.....

Moving all the joints.
1. Improvise with all the possible (and impossible) movements of your joints.

74

2. Move the space between the joints - imagine the joints having surfaces moving against each other.

c) warming-up specific body areas
Targeted warming-up of specific body parts/areas approaches: - Tension and release
- Flexibility
- Grounding
- Sensing the diagonals in the body
- Vitalising the navel as a centre of movement
- Joining the arms and legs to the centre of the body
- Anatomical lines : from the coccyx to the top of the skull.

1. The feet
Rocking the feet (Bartenieff-exercise)
(do the following exercise slowly and gently at first)
1. lie on the floor and relax. Close your eyes.
2. Your legs should be parallel and so not far apart. Press your heels gently against the floor.
3. Keeping your heels on the floor, move your toes gently forwards and backwards. Slowly increase the movement until you start rocking.
4. Let this movement travel into the whole body, through your legs, pelvis, chest and head...
5. Rock like this for a few minutes until you feel "all shook up" and relaxed.

2. The legs
moving the legs in all directions.
1. Standing, alternate your weight between the left leg and right leg
2. Move each leg playfully in all directions, find out how far you can go, how flexible you are.
3. Shake your legs in all directions
Legs against the wall
1. Lie on your back near to a wall. Put the soles of your feet against the wall and relax.

2. Straighten your legs and put them against the wall, keeping them extended.
3. Do the same but with your legs spread apart this time.
4. To finish, push yourself away from the wall!

3. The pelvis
Balancing on one point
1. Sit on the floor
2. Lift your legs and arms up into the air.
3. Shift your balance between the sit-bones.
4. Now experiment with two or three contact points. You can use your arms or legs.
5. Come back to rest and enjoy the full contact with the floor!

Moving the sacroiliac joint (the joint between the sacrum and the ilium)
1. Lie on your back and lift both knees towards your chest.
2. Roll slowly from side to side.
3. Lie on your right side. Stretch your left leg away from you without moving your other leg.
4. Repeat on the other side.

Different ways of walking
By using the whole space, try to find different ways of walking.
1. Like a bear
2. Like Marilyn Monroe
3. Like an elderly person
4. Find a new way of walking!

4. The spinal column
A stable axis from the head to the feet
1. Stand upright. Shoulders, hips and feet form a sturdy line.
2. Lean slightly forwards. Your skeleton has no problems in maintaining this upright stance.

Dolphin-wave
1. Stand loose and relaxed, your feet parallel and directly below the hip sockets. Your knees slightly bent.

2. move your pelvis forwards and backwards slightly by tipping it up and down.
3. Extend and elaborate this movement. See how the whole spine joins in and is connected to this movement.
4. Let this movement from the pelvis send a wave through the spine towards the head and back again.
5. Remain relaxed in your knees, and let this wave travel through the whole length of your body.

Letting your partner go to the floor and "shake-out"
1. Find a partner and stand opposite each other.
2. Partner B slowly sinks towards the floor while A gently holds and guides the movement.
3. Once B is on the floor, lying face up, A gently stretches and shakes the arms of B.
4. Swap roles

5. *The navel - the centre of the body*
"Belly dancing"
1. Improvise with movement around the space with your attention towards your navel which is the centre of your body.
2. The navel is the origin of the movement, the arms and legs are simply an extension from this centre.

Sensing the connections of the various parts of the body.
a) navel - head - coccyx
1. From lying down : Partner A lies down back on the floor, arms slightly above the height of the shoulders. B stretches and pulls an arm or a leg. Can you feel the bodily diagonals at work? where is the crossover point? The navel? The coccyx?
2. On all fours: round your back into a convex like a cat. Now make it concave. What is happening between your head and coccyx.
3. From standing: do some inward movement from your head towards your navel, then away from the centre away from you. Make yourself a small as you can and then as big and broad as possible.
4. While walking: feel how walking has qualities of opening and closing - while closing, imagine your head touching your navel.

b) Sensing the connection between head and navel
1. A, standing in front, places a hand onto the head of B.
2. A sends impulses into the body of B by applying little spurts of pressure through the hand. B tries to sense this impulse through to the navel or the coccyx.

Further suggestions: improvise with this exercise, using other parts of the body, other connections to the centre.

c) body crosses
1. lie on your back with your legs slightly spread out and your arms slightly above the height of the shoulders, forming an X.
2. Imagine you are a starfish, moving on the ocean floor.
3. Now, balance in this X-shape on your side.

(Arms and legs are the connection to the outside. A clear understanding of these diagonals in the body extends the movement vocabulary. If we leave this X-position while standing or lying, we become a ball, a round, flowing body!)

6. Shoulders and shoulder blades.
Talons and wings
Depending on which physical line our attention is directed towards- from the shoulder blades to the fingers - different movement images arise.

a) Talons
1. While standing, imagine holding an enormous ball in front of you.
2. The palms of your hands are towards the sky. Feel a line from your middle finger through your elbow towards your shoulder blade: a talon.
3. Improvise in space, play with the idea that you have talons....

b) Wings
1. Stand and lift your arms high and wide above your head.
2. Your hands are relaxed and slightly open. Imagine a line from the outside of your little fingers through the elbows towards your shoulder blades: your wings!
3. Move through the space - play with your wings!

Photo 24

7. Arms.

1. Swing your arm forwards away from your body. Keep repeating this movement and be aware of how this affects the rest of your body.
2. Direct your awareness towards the spatial aspects of this movement. Imagine that you have tiny flashlights on your shoulder, elbow and hand and you can see the beams of light travelling through the room.
3. Keep repeating the movement but change its pace. Maybe slowly forward then quickly back. Keep going until the movement develops its own rhythm. Can you sense any change in the movement?
4. Form a fist and push forwards against an imaginary object. Release the resistance and let the arm swing back to rest.
5. Experiment with different intensities of force. Do you feel the differences in dynamic with the different intensities?

8. Hands

Hand massage
1. Rub your hands together, using all the surfaces.
2. Using one hand, pull, squeeze and press the fingers of the other.
3. Finally, shake out your hands towards the floor.

Hand spiralling over your head
1. Stand opposite a partner and give each other a hand.

2. A moves round in one direction and B, staying in one place, turns first one way then the other.
3. The palms of your hands should be in continuous contact.

9. The head
The leading head.
1. Your head leads movement through space.
2. A partner holds your head while moving in this way. This increases the awareness of the head and helps the movement to come purely from there.

Questions:
What do I need to arrive, to land?
What parts of my body need particular attention?
How do I experience this space and the people within it?

2.1.2 Specific warming up

a) Stretching
"Pain is the body's cry for help. You are doing something which the body can no longer tolerate. The body is very patient. It needs a lot of tension and misuse before it responds with pain."[54]

Marion Rosen

Diagonal stretching in threes
1. A is lying with the back on the floor, arms slightly above the height of the shoulders, legs slightly apart (X-form). B sits next to the right arm and C next to the left leg.
2. B and C lightly pull on the diagonal created by the arm and leg, gradually creating a rhythmic swing : pull, release... pull, release...
3. After a while, B massages the fingers, hand, up to the shoulder and C the foot, calf, thigh.
4. Change to the other arm/leg and repeat

Stretching a standing partner.
1. A stands on one leg and stretches out, parallel to the floor
2. B takes hold of an arm and C a leg and both pull - gently. The spine is lightly stretched and lengthens.

80

Foto 25

b) Massage

"When we touch someone, we are touching their soul. We are not only touching their physical body. Through this outer, existential shell, we reach the entire person. We activate the flow of many different energies."[55]

Mary Whitehouse

Massage is a wonderful way of becoming mentally and physically at ease. A loosening of the musculature, a mobility of the joints and a deeper awareness of self leads to mental suppleness and physical flexibility in the movement process. So, in principle, each and every form of massage can be used. An interesting form is the Japanese "Shiatsu" which works with similar principles as contact improvisation : the giving of weight and not a forceful but flowing massage, keeping in an alert contact!

Shoulder massage and "roll down"
1. Standing with your back against a partner.
2. Let your partner massage your shoulders and arms then hold on to your pelvis.
3. Roll slowly down the spine to a forward hanging position while your partner supports the pelvis, preventing you from tipping forwards and falling.
4. Partner places a leg slightly forward so that you can sit on it.
5. Let your partner rocks you gently back and forth, from side to side by holding the sides of the pelvis.

Massage and coming to standing
1. A lies on the floor. B massages A's feet with circling movements, pulling, shaking. Then along the whole leg up to the pelvis.
2. B supports A's breathing by a gentle pressure onto the ribcage with the in-going breath and a release of pressure with the out-going breath.
3. B stretches and massages the neck of the partner.
4. B stands up by the feet of their partner and by holding onto the hands, pulls partner into a standing position.

c) Voice and breathing exercises

"A body is something wrapped around a breath. Let the wraps flow freely over one another like silk scarves."[56]

Ida Rolf

Sensing and expanding the breath.
1. A stands and sings/ hums a deep note "aaah...."
2. B places hands onto different parts of partners body: shoulders, chest, belly or back and looks for the places where they can find the most vibration.
3. A continues singing and tries to sing "into" the place of contact.

Breath and voice.
1. A sings/ hums a deep note, for instance "aaah...." and feels where in the body the strongest vibrations are.
2. Varying the tone, higher or lower, A looks for the change of location of the physical reverberations.
3. B searches manually for these places of strong vibration on A's body.
4. B touches areas of low vibration. A imagines filling these places with sound. B occasionally returns to places of strong vibration.

d) Relaxing through "Releasing"

"A Releasing alignment is not a fixed alignment; it's always in flux. Everything is relative to everything else. When its harmonious, then power and energy are released, and that becomes Releasing dance."[57]

Joan Skinner

A short example for guiding bodily relaxation in the manner of Release Technique:
"lie down on the floor.... guide your attention towards your breath ... without altering it ... simply listen and feel your breath ... with each out-going breath ... feel your flesh becoming softer ... melting along the bones ... melting from your forehead ... over your cheeks ... and your chin ... and giving its weight into the floor ... the tissue around your neck and shoulder ... melts into your arms ... down towards the fingertips ... flesh around your ribcage ... melts into the floor ... your whole body is completely loose and relaxed ..."

e) Body-Mind Centering (BMC)
". ... Organs are the primary containers or the natural habitat for our emotions, yearnings and memories of our internal response to personal history.... Body fluids represent the fluidity of movement and mind. They are the basis for presence and transformation; and through a dynamic flow mediate between rest and activity ..."

Bonnie Bainbridge Cohen

Sensing of physical chambers
Along the spine are three chambers: the abdomen, the rib-cage and the head. The following exercises draw attention to and increase awareness of these areas.

1. Filling a balloon with water
The internal chambers are filled with organs and fluids. We can use the image of a balloon, half full of water, to get a deeper understanding of how our organs and fluids behave during movement: improvise with this image though space, use different levels and speeds. What happen to the balloon when you turn? Jump? What kind of movement impulse do you receive from the balloon?

2. Hands on belly, chest, head
1. Place one of your hands onto your partner's sacrum and the other on the belly.
2. Your partner, with eyes closed, senses the space - the chamber - between your hands.
3. Repeat with the rib-cage and the head.
Further suggestions: Your partner can start to dance with you remaining in passive contact with these points.

3. Dancing with awareness directed towards the organs.

a) Abdomen: your partner with hands placed as in exercise No. 2 above, follows your dance. Try to move from the organs - do they fall when you move forwards? What is happening to them? Is it a different dance to that when you move from your muscles?

b) Rib-cage: partner places hands on sternum and upper-back - you continue your dance with awareness guided towards the organs inside this chamber ..... ?

c) Head: partner takes your head and supports its weight. Partner leads the dance by moving your head.

Guided Imagery: from the cell to a person.

Lie down with your back on the floor, relax and imagine the following:

- You are a cell. Feel your centre. You are surrounded by a warm all-embracing fluid. Through the cell membrane, nutrition filters towards you and everything the cell doesn't need is swilled away. The cell does not need to do anything - it is all taken care of.

- The single cell divides into two cells ... 4 ... 8 ... 16 ... until there is a clump of cells but still with a tangible centre - This centre becomes a navel which attaches to the placenta. Through the umbilical cord, you receive all the necessary nourishment. Again all that you don't need is swilled away.

- A head takes shape, bigger than the rump.

- Arms and legs develop, they can touch and move against the surrounding membrane

- The birth begins gently. The birth canal opens. It is tight, cramped. The head presses against it and helps its own birth.

- The lungs inflate and the breathing of air begins. The eyes open. - You begin to stretch your head towards food and your lips try to suck. - You crawl around. Gradually growing and growing, taller and taller until you stand and walk.

Mouthing

1. A lies on the floor
2. B gently strokes the corner of A's mouth, away from the centre. A follows this sensation and moves mouth and head searchingly in the direction of the stroke.
3. After a while, A slowly enlarges this movement, letting the neck and upper body stretch and turn. B supports the head and neck. Let this lead into free improvisation.

3 PHYSICAL AND EMOTIONAL SAFETY

"With contact improvisation the instincts take over: the body knows how to protect itself, because the body thinks faster than the mind"[59]

David Woodberry

In an atmosphere in which dancers can feel free to explore personal physical and emotional borders, safety plays an immense role. If we feel in safe hands emotionally, we also feel safe physically and become more daring. This also works the other way round; practising physical safety strengthens our feeling of emotional security. Physical limitations or impediments are in general not reasons to desist from dancing as the contact dancer Adwoa Lemieux describes: *"I began dancing with the limitation of one knee that wouldn't support me. The dance accounts for individual differences. My limitation was simply integrated into the dance. The process of learning the dance form was slow. I loved the movement. I slowed down and felt the sensation of my body moving. Although I had danced for many years prior to this, I began to remember the joy and simplicity of my movement. This movement had gotten lost in my formal study of dance."*[60]

The dance floor should be smooth and splinter-free to avoid injury. It is recommended when dancing outside - in a park for instance- to check for stones, shards of glass and unpleasant animal deposits! To further reduce the risk of accident, one person can take the role of "safety" and if necessary interrupt the dancing process.

Photo 26

4 Guidelines – how can I enjoy Contact Improvisation? Exercises and methods

In contact improvisation there are no guidelines to say how it should be done, only information towards safety and well-being:

Don't let yourself be victimised!

If something is uncomfortable, leave the situation and express your feelings - don't just carry on. Not being a victim is also taking responsibility for your own actions. The agreement to share your feelings, to be open about what is unpleasant, creates a freedom in itself. We can be more daring, reaching towards difficult areas of ourselves, knowing that we have a partner we can rely on for honest feedback.

Co-operation

Nobody is solely passive or active. Even when the duet comes to stillness, it should not be regarded as a problem that you have to solve. Stillness is part of your mutual process.

Giving weight is okay!

We often think that we shouldn't give weight to someone because we don't want to be a burden. On the contrary: weight is the moving force, keeps the dance flowing. We need to look for the multiplicity of weight giving options.

Not giving weight is okay too!

You don't have to give weight if you don't want to! Your partner is self-reliant and should be prepared for this.

Don't give your full weight onto specific areas

We should not give our full weight onto knees, elbows and other joints of our partner because of the risk of injury. We should avoid the face, neck and genitals as well. Different parts of the body can withstand different amounts of force.

Give your weight gradually!

This gives your partner time to react and adjust accordingly. We can transfer our weight slowly and gradually as well as a more sudden withdrawal but never at the same time. It is this combination of complete transference of weight and suddenness that causes accidents. A skill to be developed is this giving of weight by degrees, through all body parts - the larger the repertoire, the greater the freedom of choice.

Keep the flow going when taking weight!

It is important not to hinder the flow of weight when accepting it. We guide our partner towards a new shifting equilibrium - a dynamic acceptance not a static procurement! Lead/follow your partner's weight through the room, to the floor, in space, circling, spiralling.

Do as much as you can but use as little as possible!

Contact improvisation is not work. We should try to keep the use of muscle power down to a minimum as it tends to increase a wilful decision-making process. We are dealing with a relaxed, open curiosity which has a lot to do with waiting and observation.

Say yes and no!

You are not obliged to do anything in contact improvisation, there are no stipulations. You do have to dance with anyone. Be aware of your needs and be prepared to refuse an offer to dance. On the other hand - do not feel too ashamed to ask!

B EXERCISES AND METHODS

The division here between "states" and "skills" is used to simplify the structure of the following section. The solo skills are a preparation for the duet as well. The aim of all these exercises is towards the shared dance, the dialogue through movement. A perfect execution of these exercises is not the most important thing - just a playful exploration.

1 CONTACT

1.1 Contact : mental awareness states for solo dance ⎯⎯⎯

1.1.1 Relaxing

"'Tension masks sensation,' Steve Paxton has often said. The tension in the body masks the sensation of gravity, for example. You can't feel gravity, but you can feel the tension. So you relax the tension, you can feel the gravity."[61]

Nancy Stark Smith

Coming into the space and feeling the floor

1. Lie with your back on the floor and relax. Observe your breath.
2. Try to identify each and every part of your body and feel which parts are in contact with the floor and those which are "in the air".
3. Guide your attention to those parts which are in contact with the floor: buttocks, shoulder, different parts of your back, pelvis, calves, heels...
4. Consciously give your whole weight into the floor. Imagine your weight to be like the sand in an hour-glass, flowing down. With each exhalation, your breath flows through and out of your body into the floor, releasing more and more weight ...
5. End the exercise by shaking out your joints, stretching and rolling.

Questions:
- Is the floor just a strong adversary?
- Or can I get a sense of support and security from it?
- Which parts of my body are tense; which parts are relaxed?

1.1.2 Awareness of surfaces of the body

„When sitting, guide your awareness towards your body. Movement is the flow of energy, movement is above all, a vital process, because it is natural to move. We can experience a lot about ourselves. We can be aware of those senses and feelings which were unknown to us. We can increase the extent and freedom of our mobility. We can learn to trust our spontaneous responses and express them ...“[62]

Mary Starks Whitehouse

Discover the surfaces of your body

1. Roll, turn, push yourself around on the floor.
2. Touch the floor with every (possible and impossible) part of your body.

Lateral contact - up the body.

1. Stand side by side with your partner
2. Touch your partner's little toe with yours.
3. Slowly take this contact point sideways up the body - calf, knee, thigh, hips, up to the shoulders.
4. Turn around so that the other shoulder is touching.
5. Travel downwards to your little toe.

Feeling your back

1. Stand back to back with your partner but keeping about 4 inches apart. Close your eyes.
2. Feel the soles of your feet, the floor - hard, cold, soft ,warm? Give your weight into the floor, with every outward breath, give a little more. Giving weight is taking support! The floor presses upwards.
3. Slowly let your eyes open and become aware of what is around you - above, below, to the right, to the left.... in front of you....... behind.....
4. Guide your attention towards your partner - what does your back sense? Can you sense your partner's presence?

Further suggestions: slowly transfer your weight backwards until you come into contact with your partner and then gradually move to the floor.

Awakening from inside to outside

1. Stand and direct your awareness deep within you
2. Imagine a tiny animal (you) waking up inside and spreading towards the outside, through the branches of your nervous system.
3. Feel how your senses are opening, from inside your bones, through the muscles, through your skin, to the outside - start moving with this image.
4. Your awareness dilates and balloons from your body. It knows no boundaries...

Sensing the group

1. One half of the group distributes themselves around the room, stand, and close their eyes. The other half split up and stand behind someone - without touching.
2. They then gently lay their hands onto their partner's back.
3. After a while, they remove their hands and walk to someone else ......

Questions:
- Is the outer limit of my body the surface of my skin?
- How did I experience my partner?
- How do I sense my self?
- Did I feel the other person?
- Did I notice any differences between the people?

1.1.3 Strengthening the emotional sense

"Suppression and counteraction are the most common tactics that we use to protect our hearts, the normal characteristics preventing us from getting in touch with our vulnerability, our compassion and from our sense for the open and fresh dimension of being. Through suppression and counteraction we sanction suffering, dismay and confusion."[63]

Pema Chödrön

In order to dance contact improvisation with someone, the emotions emerging from the dance have to be acknowledged and respected. Even though there is no special agreement made between the dancers, it is a matter of course that we provide an emotional support for our partner. the prerequisite here is that we are able to recognise our own feelings and emotional states. This is not as simple as we might imagine. A lot of people rationalise the feelings - especially when talking about them. We should be looking for a playful way of dealing with them, as Ruth Zaporah describes:*"Their greatest joy [the students] was that they could play with intensive emotions. Feelings are toys with which you can play. To understand that can be extremely useful, especially when we consider emotions often have an immense power over us, even becoming their victims."*[64]

The yes-and-no exercise
1. A touches B with one hand somewhere on the body and says, "Yes"; B always responds to the touch with "No".
2. A keeps on touching and saying yes; B takes time, senses the touch, reactions, feelings, images and then says No! (...because it's the exercise!)
3. After a while, let this lead into free improvisation, with no limitations on verbalisation ...

Clarification: even when the "No" should be "Yes" and vice versa, it is interesting to stick to the rules of this exercise. It can release strong emotions, memories and reactions though and should be practised with the principal of self-responsibility - don't be forced into anything, be aware of your personal borders. Make clear to your partner what is emotionally acceptable at that moment.

The "circle of connected hearts"
1. Everyone sits in a circle - in silence.
2. Each places their right hand over their hearts and the left hand onto the shoulder of the person sitting on the left.
3. Helpful affirmative statements to be spoken can be: "We open our hearts to each other", "We meet each other openly and honestly" "We are here free from prejudice and intolerance."

Questions:
- how do I handle my feelings?
- Do I act neutrally?
- Do I allow myself feelings? Suppress them? If so, how do I suppress them?

1.1.4 To be both active and passive

"Toil without exertion"[65]

Karlfried Graf Dürckheim

Active and passive means here: developing a balance between sensing and doing. This is a major difference to both ballet and modern dance where the active doing is at the forefront. It is often the case in contact improvisation that we should do nothing, rather wait, remaining open and present to what is, an active lingering for the next movement impulse. The main activity in contact improvisation is in essence, mindfulness, sensing and collecting information.

Perhaps the division between "being" and "doing", active and passive, is made out of habit - with a little practice we can discover their unity while dancing. This can be done while walking too: be mindful of your feet touching the floor and at the same time be aware of your surroundings, the world in all its aspects, around you.

The puppet
1. Lie relaxed on the floor and let your partner move you.
2. Your partner takes your legs, arms, hips, head, etc., and places you into as many different positions as possible - you remain relaxed and passive.
3. After a while, you start to move with the manipulation of your partner and "help".
4. You become increasingly more active until you find a balance between "being" and "doing"
5. Slowly swap roles until your partner is lying passively on the floor.......

Active and passive simultaneously
1. Lie relaxed on the floor and let your partner move and lead you.

2. Through gentle yet clear directional pressure from your partner's hands, you start to move; the dance can start from the floor and lead to standing. You are not like a sack of potatoes but let yourself be led which means a certain amount of activity.
3. After a while swap roles.....

Questions :
- Do I prefer the active or the passive role?
- What is attractive about this particular role?
- What am I afraid of when I'm in the other role?

1.1.5 Risk taking

"Accept your limits. I ask that students allow themselves the permission to realize their limitations. I also encourage the sudden stretch beyond limitations. To see within this language the existence of a subtle yet expansive definition to the word 'Risk'."[66]

Alan Ptashek

In every phase of contact improvisation it is possible to go that one step further and try out something new. This opens up the whole spectrum of physical as well as emotional mobility and is sometimes fun as well. It certainly is very exciting!

This is not an recommendation for indiscrimination and recklessness. The biggest risk maybe is to allow a real "meeting" to take place - courageously permitting confrontations. Far away from the tendency to look for comfort and avoid adversity.

One way of working with risk-taking is to practise falling: falling through the room, suddenly letting go of your weight into the floor. Uncertainty can get rid of the fear of losing control - and is a good opportunity to work with the unfamiliar....

Being prepared to take risks means as well, taking responsibility for your own safety, making sure hands and arms are free to come to the rescue in emergencies. The amount of trust placed in the earth determines the magnitude of risk-taking!

Try something new
1. Consider things that you are afraid of while dancing: falling, being upside down, dynamic...?
2. Work with a partner on these areas, allow yourself to explore these fearful situations.

Further suggestions:
- Watch other dancers, look for new ideas and qualities which you can try out.
- ask someone to dance, who you have previously avoided.
- consciously take your body towards new movement qualities, be dynamic if you have a tendency to be smooth and even, be demanding and direct if you feel you are normally too considerate.......

Questions:
- Which positions do I find peculiar?
- Do I take risks? When? how? where?
- Am I prepared to catch myself?
- What do I need to be able to take these risks?

1.2 Contact : Awareness states in duets _____

1.2.1 Allowing encounters

"In the beginning is the relationship: as a category of being, as a readiness, tangibility, a model of the soul; imperative to relationships : the inherent 'thou'."[67]

Martin Buber

What happens during the moment of encounter between two people and how it is experienced is impossible to predict: we can be open to the situation and be astonished. It is about sensing and experiencing what is really happening between your partner - forgetting preconceived notions and letting the moment be the judge. It is about letting go of sympathy/ antipathy assumptions. What is actually happening in this encounter? Let yourself be surprised!

Meeting your partner
1. A and B stand facing each other, about 4 or 5 metres apart. 2. At the same time, they take a step towards each other and freeze in a spontaneous pose.
3. Going back to the original positions, they repeat the step with different poses.
4. End the exercises with feedback: how did I feel? What was happening between us?
Variations: increase the encounter by extending the poses into short sequences and brief movement dialogues.
When two people meet, it can have many different qualities: for, against, with, without, on, in, under, between, through.......

Closeness and distance: saying "Stop!"
1. A few pieces of clothing mark out a "stage". A and B stand at opposing sides of the stage.
2. A moves slowly towards B. B says " Stop!" when A has come "near enough".
3. Both try to sense what this distance feels like: was it easy for me to say stop? Did I say it too late? Why did my partner say stop at that moment? ....

Dancing in circles and making "contact"
This exercise is about getting eye contact with each member of the group. One way is a free improvisation in two circles - people with the same colour socks for instance form the outer circle and the rest the inner. Other variations : all the men dance on the outside........

The way we achieve this eye to eye contact tells us a lot about ourselves and our partner. what qualities did this contact possess? Reticence? Brashness? Nervous? Insincere? Exciting? Aggressive? Playful?

Questions:
- How does it feel "to be in contact with myself"?
- What kind of choices do I make when I look for a partner?
- How do I make contact? Am I open or only pretending?
- Do I reject contact or do I search for it?
- Is this a verbal or physical process?
- Was the physical contact pleasant? Where wasn't it?

1.2.2 Having goals and letting them go

"Stop these unnecessary speculations, you have made hundreds of plans which have never been realised and only lead to frustration. Incomplete deeds are like splashing of waves. Remain with yourself and stop making your head spin."[68]

Chögyam Trungpa

Contact improvisation is a constant shifting of aims, between persistence and vacillation, a decisive quandary, accepting the mutual reality in order to stay in the improvisation. Without aims, the dance would soon become boring, for they give direction and energy to the dance. But with wilful persistence, the dance becomes rigid and turns into a jostling match. We have to prepared for continual directional change to stay with the movement flow. What we are finally looking for are shared decisions, letting us do as much as possible with the least effort.

Head to head towards the floor
1. Partners stand together and touch heads - foreheads, back of the heads ......
2. Both give weight into this contact point and keeping together, search for a way to the floor.
3. Keeping in contact, find a way back to standing.

Questions:
- Am I thinking a lot while I dance? If so, does it affect my dancing / my awareness of my partner?
- Am I ambitious while I am dancing?
- Do I notice if my partner is not really "there" when we dance together?
- Is it possible to simultaneously "do what I want " and to " want nothing"?

1.2.3 Leading and Following

"There is a give and take of weight, but also of social roles, of passiveness and activeness, of demand and response. The goal is to find the easiest pathways available to the mutually moving masses"[69]

Steve Paxton

Letting yourself be led is often not very easy and can produce varying reactions: fear of losing control and authority or inversely relief that decisions are taken out of your hands for a while! Being led can lead to new experiences: leading doesn't mean necessarily domination. If no-one leads, there is no direction!

If a strong resistance to being led surfaces during dancing, the following points can be discussed: the leader is maybe too adamant in approach, leading to a natural physical resistance in the partner and ends with the duet becoming a trial of wills (which is normal in daily life!). The one being led can integrate these feelings into the dance, by an open acceptance as well as a positive experimentation within the improvisation (Try sharp or viscous movement for example).

Leading a partner on the floor
1. A lies on the floor, eyes closed, in an embryonic position. B places hands onto A.
2. A slowly starts to move.
3. B follows the movement by touching and supporting.
4. B then starts to initiate movement by gentle pressure and leads/follows A around the room.

Move your partner and offer resistance
1. Stand behind your partner.
2. Place your hands onto your partner's shoulders or back.
3. Slowly move, swing, shake ...... your partner.
4. After a while your partner starts to move independently. Go with the movement and occasionally offer resistance to the movement, sometimes even stop the movement. Can your grade or dose your resistance?

(Not) using your hands
Special attention should be given to your hands. As a rule of thumb, as a beginner try not to use your hands to grip onto your partner, don't hold onto arms or legs - this ensures that your partner has the maximum mobility and freedom. It also greatly reduces the risk of injury! As Curt Siddall remarks:"The hands are de-emphasised to about the same utility as the foot; a means of support at the end of the arm and a linear extension of the movement in the arm ..... the hands never grab. This

type of action is a natural response for a beginner, but is simply too dangerous and painful to one's partner. Relaxed fingers and the use of every square inch of the body as a contact surface or "handle" is the sign of an experienced contact improviser."[70]

Don't take contact improvisation into your own hands!

Conscious avoidance of arms and hands
1. Dance with a partner
2. Do not touch each other with your arms or hands. Dance with an active disavowal of these limbs.

Questions:
- Do I find it easier to lead or follow? Why?
- What happens when my partner doesn't follow my movement?
- Are we really dancing together?
- Has communication between us become clearer?

1.2.4 The value of disorientation

"Disorientation must become an acceptable sensation. A released body, supported in length, can be developed. Trust, patiently nurtured through confidence and familiarity, prepares the way for diversity. Through trust, awkward, uncomfortable moments of vulnerability and powerful moments of virtuosity become equally rich"[71]

Randy Warshow

There are often positions and movement sequences in contact improvisation which are not customary and literally turn things upside down! Hanging with your head near the floor, falling backwards, turning in the air. All these things can cause a certain disorientation which may give rise to fear. But there are a few advantages as well. You may find yourself doing surprising things, movement habits vanish. Unplanned "holes" in the movement flow may appear, moments of uncertainty or monotony which increase the awareness of the here-and-now, for the actuality of the moment. If these moments are not eradicated through forced activity, we may find ourselves in a more authentic contact with the continually changing situation - contact improvisation!

Giving weight backwards
1. A stands about a pace behind B
2. A puts hands onto the shoulders of B
3. Keeping the body straight and toned, B leans back into the support of A.

Further suggestions: A stands behind B but without touching. A says "Okay!" telling B that it is okay to fall backwards and be caught by A.

Questions:
- Do I get easily irritated?
- What irritates me exactly?
- How can I tell what the "moment" is offering me - and what it is not?

1.3 Physical skills for solo dance

1.3.1 Sensing your own mass

"There's a kind of directness in relationship to your body as physical entity - you have weight, you have a skeleton, and, if you arrange it properly, it will be easier to move. You're putting your body on the line, and there's some risk involved, some awareness of safety, and contact with the forces of gravity and momentum - feeling them, really feeling them, feeling totally swept over by them..."[72]

Nancy Stark Smith

In order to give our weight, we first have to have a sense of our weight - feeling the forces of nature and their influence on our movement. We can experience gravity through contact with the floor for instance, (without a floor there would be no experience of weight!).

The dancers receive information about their "state" through touch. We sense the amount of weight given and the way it is given through our skin and body surfaces and also our own readiness to take weight. That is why there are a lot of exercises in contact improvisation about playing with weight using different parts of the body, controlling, dosing, shifting... We can also learn to make our weight lighter or heavier!

a) Dancing while standing still - The Small Dance

Simply standing still with your awareness directed inwards, towards your physical state is already be a little "dance", for standing is not something fixed and rigid but a lively dance of balance. There is a continual interplay between the musculature and the skeleton. Minuscule corrections which are often invisible from the outside, keep the body upright in a stable flowing balance.

The following exercise makes us aware of these subtle inner movements of our body, it allows us to sense the pull of gravity while we are standing steadily on the earth. We allow our weight to sink into the earth through our feet.

The following text is from *Steve Paxton*, who introduced the practice of the Small Dance into contact improvisation:

"It's a fairly easy perception: all you have to do is stand up and then relax ... and at a certain point you realise that you've relaxed everything that you can relax but you're still standing and in that standing is quite a lot of minute movement..... the skeleton holding you upright even though you're mentally relaxing... Call it the "small dance".... it was a name chosen largely because its quite descriptive of the situation and because while you're doing the stand and feeling the "small dance" you're aware that you're not doing it, so, in a way, you're watching yourself perform its function. And your mind is not figuring anything out and not searching for any answers or being used as an active instrument but is being used as a lens to focus on certain perceptions."[73]

Nancy Stark Smith describes the same phenomenon in a slightly different way: *"Align your skeleton along the forces of gravity, sending your weight evenly down through your bones back to the earth. Remember the center of the earth, its density. Empty of idea, full of sensation, feel the small dance, the delicate inner balancing act of a 2-legged creature; falling gently on and off center, weaving about your axis. Feel the rise of the earth's strength back through your bones, supporting your stand"*[74]

When standing or "small dancing", we can get a sense of a vertical ease, a condition in which the skeleton is in equilibrium and the muscles are not "trying" to sustain our position.

101

b) The floor as support

Contact improvisation allows us to rediscover the supportive nature of the floor. Through the creation of a direct and conscious relationship with it, we get a feeling of stability and "grounding" ("partnering with the ground" (Paxton)). On an emotional level, we feel secure and self-assured. It is only possible to stand with the support of the floor, its resistance. This becomes clearer when repeatedly standing and falling: the up and down becomes a mutual dependence, it connects the pressure needed to stand with the release when falling. The floor becomes your partner!

Photo 27

The floor as partner
1. Lie with your belly on the floor.
2. Feel which parts of your body are in contact with the floor and those which are not.
3. Prop yourself up from the floor, with your arm or leg for example. Then relax again.
4. Repeat the same action but this time relaxing into a different position.
5. Find out more about the supportive and bracing qualities of the floor.

Questions:
-   How do I give my weight to the floor?
-   Is it clear how the natural forces, gravity for instance, are working for and not against me?
-   How do I normally move, day to day? Have I changed my movement patterns since doing contact improvisation ?

1.3.2 Moving your mass

"Contact is a movement form that feeds into the positive, balanced, reasonable side of human nature but does not deny the demonic. It gives permission for deep sensitivity but balances that with the ultimate realities of physical laws - gravity, momentum, inertia"[75]

Emily Ransom

a) A slow shift of weight

It is easy to give your whole weight at once as well as giving no weight. In some respects, contact improvisation addresses these childhood desires for dependence. In a more mature form they can develop into a conscious self-abandon. A slow shifting of weight makes it easier for the partner to support and is also a lot safer. In this context it is important to experience the numerous gravitational axes that the body has, not only standing up and lying down, because weight is always transformed by movement. We meet various aspects of these forces:

-   Gravity: a downwards pull.
-   Centripetal force: a sideways pull towards the centre
-   Weight in the centre
-   Weight off centre

"Filling and emptying" body parts

a slow transference of weight means to be able to give weight in a controlled and conscious way. We could describe it as filling the different parts of our body with weight (heavier) or emptying (lighter). This skill makes it easier to achieve soft and flowing movement with your partner.

Filling and emptying your legs with sand

1. Choose a place in the room, go there and come to an easy standing.
2. Share your weight evenly between both feet. Your knees are loose and slightly bent. Your shoulders are relaxed and you are in a good vertical posture. Observe but don't change your evenly flowing breath.
3. Guide your attention inwards. Feel the floor beneath your feet. What does it feel like? Soft, cold, hard, warm.....?
4. Be aware of the structure of your skeleton, from your feet to your skull. Your skeleton is carrying your whole weight. Consciously let go of as much muscular support as possible. Let as much weight flow into the ground as you can without losing your upright stability.
5. Notice the small movements, small adjustments your body makes to keep you standing.
6. Initiate a tiny stretch with your left arm towards the floor, and then let it come back to where it was. Sense it, feel what is happening. Stretch again but even smaller... repeat with your right arm.
7. Slowly shift your weight into your right leg then back through the middle and into the left leg. Feel the weight emptying from one leg and filling the other, like sand in an hourglass.
8. Start to sway slightly. Slowly increase this shift of weight until you fall to the side. Take a few steps and return to standing. Repeat.

b) Sensing and shifting the point of contact

Here the point of contact is the parts of the body which touch your partner (not the floor).

We can make the following distinctions:

1. Size: contact through a point or a larger surface
2. Place: contact with one body part or more.
3. Manner: rotating or lineal contact (turning around each other or sliding for instance).

In the following exercise the point of contact should remain as small as possible and most importantly: maintain consistent contact, don't slide away from or avoid any body surface.

A wall as partner
1. Lean with your back to the wall. Your feet are slightly apart.
2. Slowly give your weight into the wall - though your hips, sacrum. Once you feel that your weight is transferring, shift the point of contact up through your back into your shoulders and back down again.
3. Come away from the wall and slowly and gently return your weight to the wall.
4. With your contact point, write your name on the wall ... or paint a picture...
5. Roll vertically along the wall. Without arms and legs the roll becomes rounder and softer. Are there gaps or holes in the point of contact?
6. Take the point of contact into your head or arms. Move up and down with the wall.

Questions:
- Can I let go and give my weight? What does it feel like?
- How does my contact point feel? Hard, sharp, soft, fluid?
- What do I want from my partner? what do I expect?

1.3.3 Rolling

"...... the human body has corners, but to stay in permanent contact it is necessary to round them off. That is the only way to get harmonious and organic movement. If our upper bodies are turning around each other, it's best to get rid of the arms because then the edges disappear....."[76]

Ulla Brinkmann

Probably not many people have rolled around on the floor a lot since their childhood. The following exercises give suggestions for rolling, how different parts of the body can initiate rolls. It is very important when rolling to remain soft and relaxed, keeping the body round and to enjoy it!

105

a) Rolling alone

1. Rounding the body

as mentioned before, it's important to keep the body round so that we avoid painful knees, elbows and other joints.

Round like a ball.

Improvise, imagining you are a ball. Arms, legs, spine become as round as a ball and roll about the room.

Two balls roll around each other
1. Both partners place their arms as if carrying a large ball. Hands, elbows, upper arm and shoulder form a large semicircle.
2. Starting from the fingertips, roll around each other.

Photo 28

2. Rolling on the floor
Rolling and circling on the floor
1. Sit on the floor, the soles of your feet together, hold onto your feet

Photo 29

106

2. Roll to the side, make a circle and come up on the other side.
3. Crouch down on your toes. Place your hands on the floor to the side of you, lift yourself up and swing.

Backwards roll
1. Crouch down on your toes.
2. Slowly put your bottom on the floor and roll backwards over your back.
3. Roll backwards over a shoulder. Important tip: it is very helpful to keep both hands close to your head, to support your neck and push yourself up. This protects the upper vertebrae as well!

Further suggestions: roll diagonally backwards over the left or right shoulder. Return by rolling forwards using the diagonal right shoulder - left buttock or left shoulder - right buttock.

An elephant lolling about in the mud
1. Lie down on your back. Let your arms and legs relax and shut your eyes.
2. Loll about on the floor, stretch, turn, roll. Imagine you have just woken up and don't need to get up quite yet........ imagine you are an elephant in a cool pool of slimy mud.

Rolling along your longitudinal axis.
Rolling comes from an invisible shift of weight inside the centre of the body. The lifting of an arm or a leg from the floor while rolling can happen primarily from the shifting of weight and not muscular force.

a) Hands support the roll
This preparatory exercise develops a more intensive sense of weight shift and helps in relaxing.

1. A rolls around the room freestyle. B places hands onto any parts of A's body which happen to be facing up.
2. B gives weight through the hands, through A, vertically down towards the floor. B should not hinder A but rather help A with this extra weight, to get a clearer sense of the shifting of weight.

Rolling on the floor with an extended body can be initiated from various parts of the body.

b) The arms lead the roll
1. Lie relaxed with your back on the floor. Your hands are next to your body.
2. With your left arm, stroke your right shoulder, down your right arm past your fingertips, onto the floor and further... the rest of your body follows and you end up rolling onto your front.

Photo 30

3. Keep rolling, your left arm stroking down your right side all the time.
4. Practice with your right arm as initiator. Improvise and find new ways to start rolling with your hands or arms.

c) The feet lead the roll
1. Lie relaxed with your back on the floor.
2. Lead your left foot down your right leg, past your toes, onto the floor and keep stretching in this direction. The rest of your body follows and you are on your belly.
3. Keep going , your left leg leading all the time.
4. Practice with your right leg, improvise, find variations.....

Further suggestions: let your pelvis initiate a roll to the side......

d) The banana roll
1. Lie down on your back and relax. Turn slowly to one side. Curve yourself into a banana with your torso and legs coming slightly forwards.

108

2. Slowly start to turn,
    trying to keep this
    slight curvature.
    Good luck!

Photo 31:
The banana roll

b) Rolling with support
Turning the head and holding the belly
1. A leans back against B
2. B takes a careful hold of A's head
    and belly
3. B starts rocking movements with A
    then turns A's head and Belly
    towards the floor. A rolls away
    from the floor and B leans back
    against ......

Photo 32 : Rolling with support

Rolling between the legs
1. A stands with legs apart, B is curled up beneath them.
2. A begins to roll B like a ball. Mostly use the inside of your legs....

Questions:
- Did I find smooth transitions when rolling?
- Do I like turning or do I tend to avoid it?
- Have I found my movement, my dance?

Photo 33: Rolling between the legs.

1.3.4 Spiralling

"..... when someone learns contact improvisation, they have to learn to accept disorientation..... moving through space in spirals and curves, and not in straight lines - like most of our day-to-day movement"[77]

Cynthia J. Novack

Moving down towards the floor
1. Turn around the centre of your body.
2. Reach out an arm towards the floor and support yourself with the palm of your hand.
3. Your body turns downwards in a spiral towards the floor, first your knee touches the ground, then your thigh....... keep turning your body on the floor.

Further suggestions: spiral towards the floor with a partner.

Turning on one leg
1. You are standing
2. Lift and stretch a leg.
3. Use the stretched leg to turn and go down to the floor.
4. Walk around the room, turn and roll into the floor from jumping.

Questions:
1. Do I become disoriented when I am turning?
2. Do I lose my balance easily?
3. How do I perceive momentum when I am turning?

1.3.5. Falling and moving off-centre

"Contact, the anti-system of the art of moving, soft, warm, round, intelligent....attentive, and supple as a cat, who always lands on her feet after falling and never hurts herself"[78]

Omar - after his first Contact weekend-workshop

Contact improvisation is a dance of falling: in a duet, both dancers fall into a mutual centre, which is always influenced by gravity. We work with gravity and falling as the decisive forces. Falling means moving away from the centre of gravity, because every time we are off-centre we are forced to move. Ballet and modern dance use falling as well but only as a transition to the next movement. Contact improvisation uses it to create a continuous movement. Contact dancers fall towards a common gravitational centre, meet and often fall towards the floor. To achieve a satisfactory dance together it is necessary to find, from the beginning, ways and opportunities of moving, using as little energy as possible.

Falling can cause dizziness and nausea. To reduce the likelihood of such reactions, it is best to avoid falling too quickly, and to 'soft focus' your eyes by not keeping your vision fixed on one place. The most important point is probably to be relaxed and allow yourself to become disoriented. It takes time to get away from a visual orientation, which can denote security and control, towards a physical, kinaesthetic orientation.

Falling and standing up
1. Move slowly around the room : on your feet, hands, arms - all possible (and impossible) ways.....
2. Find yourself moving towards the floor, sometimes away from the floor, on the floor and up again to standing.
3. Find out how your weight goes to the floor - use all of your surface.

Photo 34: (Photo: Archiv Scott Wells)

In this exercise, we can find out how the ground accepts our weight and through its resistance, makes standing upright possible. "It is a deliberate and patient journey", as Steve Paxton describes, because ".. the giving is where the play comes. There's you and the room to play with"[79]

Discover different pathways
1. Move freely around the room
2. Find different ways of coming to the floor.
3. Repeat 3 ways
Further suggestions: teach your 3 ways to a partner. learn your partner's 3 ways.

Sinking and turning
1. Face your partner and hold hands
2. Shake and loosen each other's arms.
3. A lets B slowly down towards the floor, offering a slight resistance.
4. A lets B fall onto the side and starts to spin them on the side.
5. B turns, pulls knees up and uses the momentum to come to kneeling.

Questions:
- Do I fall hard or soft onto the floor? Why?
- What am I feeling when I'm falling?
- how can I connect the states of deep relaxation and extreme alertness?

1.3.6 Jumping

"...... don't do anything if your partner jumps badly.... don't try to hold on, just offer a direction but don't force it!"[80]

Scott Wells

Preliminary exercise: skating through the room
1. Imagine the floor is ice and you're skating through the room. Woollen socks are useful!
2. Use the sides of your feet to slide, experiment with turning.

Swing and jump
1. Warm your feet up to prepare by repeatedly rolling them from the toes to the heels and back again.
2. From standing, using the weight of your arms, swing your torso down towards your knees and back up again, letting your heels lift from the floor.
3. Without adding any muscular force, increase the swing's momentum by taking a deep breath with the upwards movement. Let the momentum carry you off the floor, your feet seemingly leaving the floor by themselves!
4. The spine remains aligned and supports the jump. Land softly through your toes onto your feet.

Photo 35

Jumping through space
1. Move freely through the room.
2. Try out various jumps: forwards, backwards, to the side, with one leg, turning.......keep control!

Frog leaps
1. Crouch down, hands on the floor.
2. Jump and hop through the room like a frog. Keep your pelvis low and your legs spread wide.

Rolling and jumping with support
1. Move around the room. Crouch down on your toes, roll onto your back, swing forward and jump up.
2. Let two people help and support your jump by placing their arms under yours and lift you up higher.

Questions:
- What is it like, being high up?
- Is it easy for me to leave the floor for a moment?
- How do I land on the floor? Hard? Soft?

Photo 35a

2 CONTACT: DUET SKILLS

2.1 Maintaining a point of contact with a partner————

"Contact Improvisation is sensitizing the body to the elements that make movement happen. It's standing, lifting, falling and rolling in physical contact with a partner at all times"[81]

Nancy Stark Smith

The point of contact between the surfaces of our bodies should be continually shifting. A rolling shift, not slipping or jumping. The contact point will remain together as long as both dancers continuously give weight.

Keeping the point of contact.
1. Stand back to back with a partner with the focus of contact at the sacrum.
2. Slowly shift weight to the sacrum. See the weight as sand pouring in to fill the sacrum. You can pour a lot at once too! Be mindful. What is the difference between shifting a lot or a little sand?
3. Let the contact point travel upwards towards the shoulders and back down again to the pelvis. Bring the rest of your body into play.
4. Become more and more playful. Let it go into a open improvisation. let go of the exercise and simply follow what is happening between you, your weight and your partner.....

Points of contact in groups of three
1. A stands in between B and C and is in physical contact with both.
2. B and C are not touching but still dance together, A being the point of contact between them, the communicative duct, information about weight, direction, pressure passing through.

Foot Dance
1. Sit on the floor
2. Wriggle your toes
3. Rotate your ankle, letting your toes draw a big circle in the air.

4. Rub, press, clap your feet together.
5. One foot leads you through the room, your body follows with soft and flowing movement.

Further suggestions: let your foot find a partner and improvise a Foot Dance.

A footbridge
1. A and B lie down with feet touching.
2. Both press away from the floor, creating a "foot-bridge"
3. Try different positions, play with going to the side, turning......

Photo 36

Finding your partners head
1. Both partners sit opposite each other on the floor. Lean forward slightly and using their heads, try to come into contact with their partners.
2. Both partners stand opposite each other, about an arm's length away. Keeping eyes closed, use your head to find your partners head. When in contact, give a little weight to the point of contact and then go back to standing. Repeat.

The bodywave
1. Stand head to head with your partner.
2. Give a little weight to this contact point, keeping in contact, move carefully forwards and backwards. Your body should be soft and relaxed.
3. The giving and taking of weight can create a kind of physical wave in your body. Feel how your weight goes through your partner into the floor. Feel the floor through your partners head.

Head dance
1. Place your forehead onto your partners head.
2. Slowly roll your head around, explore all movement potential.
3. Start to move your whole body, change directions and stance. Keep in contact through the head.

Further suggestions: instead of the head of your partner, choose a different place to keep contact with - you could even choose to use the floor.

Holding your partners head while dancing.
1. Lie with your back on the floor and relax.
2. Your partner cradles your head with the hands and starts to gently rock and move it around.
3. After a while your partner leads you from your head to standing. Begin a head dance, your partner supporting your dance through this hand-head contact.

Questions:
- How do I approach the first moment of contact?
- Am I really using all the possible areas of my body for contact? - Can I stay in a continual contact?

2.2 Giving of weight

"There's a kind of directness in relationship to your body as a physical entity – you have weight, you have a skeleton, and, if you arrange it properly, it will be easier to move"[82]

Nancy Stark Smith

It is important in contact improvisation to abandon the security of verticality and let the body experience as many different directions of gravitational "pull" as possible. Placing your weight horizontally onto your partner for instance, or let weight fall down and away in counterbalancing. The head dance offers the chance to experience and experiment with these lines of gravity. The interplay of weight and balance can be looked at in three ways:

1. The amount of weight given - ranging through touching just enough to trigger the nerves, a light lean, giving the weight of one body part and, giving your whole weight.
2. The amount of weight taken - ranging through the first perception of touch, accepting and giving in to the weight and, replying with equal force (taking weight).
3. The ways and means of giving and taking weight (pull/push).

2.2.1 Touch means: give a little weight

"As Flow does not mean slow, receptivity needn't be measured by passivity. 'Listening' is one of my favourite words in describing the force behind transition"[83]

Alan Ptashek

Depending on the magnitude, touch reaches different levels of ourselves: skin, muscle, bone as well as the different "psycho-energetic" states of awareness. When we stimulate our skin through touch, stroking, caressing or through muscle activity, we receive sensual feedback about our physical surface and therefore our a sense of ourselves as an individual. The "light touch exercise" from Nancy Stark Smith gives us an insight into this area. During the 'light touch' dance, the touch remains light and fleeting but with a continual flowing point of contact.

Variations
1. You are standing. Your partner places a hand somewhere on your body.
2. Both of you now give a little weight into this contact point. After a while, transfer the weight back but remain in contact.

3. Repeat and let it develop into a duet, swapping roles....

Photo 37

2.2.2 Finding your physical limits

"Feel the earth under the feet of the other - that's real contact"[84]

Scott Wells

We can practise the "filling and emptying" of weight with a partner. The one taking the weight has the task of taking as much weight as is comfortable, keeping relaxed and guiding the weight of the partner in a downwards flow to the floor. Here, the dancers also learn how much weight specific body parts, such as the knee, can take. It is often surprising to find how resilient and sturdy our body really is. Remember - use your skeleton as support, not muscle power!

Crawling over your partner
1. Your partner lies face down on the floor
2. Begin crawling carefully over your partner, keeping contact light.
3. Gradually increase the weight through your hands onto your partners body - arms, legs, back etc. Your partner tells you when it becomes uncomfortable.
4. Try sitting and lying on your partner to find out how much weight is possible.

Further suggestions: the whole group starts crawling, sliding, rolling, at different speeds around the room. Accidental contact within the group leads eventually to a large seething mass of bodies crawling, sitting, lying on one another.

2.2.3 Giving your whole weight

"Learning by doing"[85]

John Dewey

The sacrum game

1. Let the point of contact with your partner be your sacrum.
2. Gently pour weight into this contact point.
3. Slowly lift a leg and play around with it.
4. Gradually turn around your partner, letting the point of contact wander.

Photo 38

Giving weight through a large surface.

1. Start a duet
2. Gradually focus your attention on giving your weight through large surfaces - keep mindful of your partner.

Photo 39: ContactArt 1995 in "Momentaufnahme"
L. Stephan, N. Heckelei, I. Uderstädt, M. Treinies
(from Moving Arts) (Photo: Holger Gruss)

Leading weight through the room.

1. Stand behind your partner
2. Your partner slowly gives weight backwards. Accept it and give it back.

3. Repeat but this time take the weight and guide it into another part of the room.

Weight on the top of your feet
1. Crawl on your hands and feet.
2. Place most weight through your hands and do small jumps, landing gently onto the top of your extended feet.

2.2.4 "Clamping" and carrying

"If we remember to see the other as unique accumulations of energy, unfixed and dynamic, seeing becomes a medium for self-renewal. if we can reflect this intelligence back to one another, whatever our momentary form, we become easily accessible resources for each other"[86]

Deborah Hay

Clamping practise
1. Start a dance with your partner
2. The task moves to exploring the possibilities of clamping yourself onto the body of your partner ... with your legs, arms, head ...... Keep it playful and don't use your hands.

Holding the neck
1. Stand behind your partner
2. Support your partners neck with your hands, letting your partner lean backwards.
3. Keeping your partners weight, change your "grip". It is like climbing - make sure the new grip is safe before letting the other one go. Further suggestions: both partners hold each other's necks, heads, etc. and begin to dance.

Become a clothes-peg
1. Stand opposite your partner
2. Lift your arm and place your armpit onto your partners shoulder. Let your arm fall diagonal down the back of your partner so that your weight is evenly distributed through your partners spine.
3. Your partner can now straighten up and carry you through the room.
Variation: jump into this "peg" position.

Photo 40

Clamping and "carry the baby"
1. Stand opposite your partner and lift your lower arms in front of you by bending your elbows.
2. Your partner "does the clothes-peg" but lifts the inside leg into your arms as well.
3. Without jumping, your partner lifts the other leg into your arms and at the same time, twists the pelvis inwards towards the centre. This makes it a lot easier to carry.
4. Carry your baby through the space.
Variation : pass the baby on to different people.

2.2.5 Climbing

"It can be helpful to talk about support but a direct physical experience of it is often a lot clearer"[87]

Rim Nov

Tree climbing
1. Stand solid and stable as a tree
2. Let your partner climb you, and with your support, trying out as many ways as possible to clamp, climb, hook onto you.

Climbing in a forest

One person is the monkey, the rest of the group are trees. The monkey travels from tree to tree, trying to find as much support and as much surface contact as possible. The trees are again active in the support for the monkey - arboreal symbiosis!

Example for 3 participants:
1. A climbs onto B and C, using one contact point per person as more than one can lead to instability or it is simply too much for one tree!
2. A changes position continually while B and C support. A tries to stay off the ground as long as is possible.

Photo 41:

Questions:
- How much weight can I give before I become afraid?
- Do I get a real feeling of support from my partner?
- How do I build up trust?

2.3 Support: taking weight

"Falling, carrying, lifting, balancing, rolling - use gravity in your movement, accept impulses...... the spectrum ranges from soft meditative movement through to a rollicking athletic dance. Why? To immerse into a new, harmonious movement experience."[88]

Rusty Lester

Support is a central theme in contact improvisation. Not just its "carrying" aspect but more as springboard for new notions of movement. It is important to remember that you always have freedom of choice whether to take weight or not and if so, how much; taking more weight means taking more responsibility. As mentioned before, even though there are no previously defined agreements between the dancers, it is taken for granted that your partner is physical and emotionally supportive, lessening the risk of injury or negative experience. We are sometimes surprised when offering support, how much more resilient we are than previously suspected - this discovery of strength increases self-confidence. On the other side though, it is important to learn the limits of how much weight we can take.

If you want to "get rid of" weight or finish the duet, find ways to carefully lead your partner to the floor. The roles of giver and taker should be shifting continuously. The taking of weight can take place through:
- *Posting (offering surfaces)*
- *Sloughing (leaning and slithering off)*
- *Weight rolling on the body (body-surfing)*

2.3.1 Posting
You can offer your partner various surfaces of support: on all fours like a bench, or standing, knees bent and leaning forward (table) or simply the sides of your body.

a) Bench
You often find yourself being neither up nor down but in the midrange, spatially when improvising, positions which offer a whole range of movement.: on all fours the back can become a "bench", giving your partner a large surface of support. With practise, new elements can be introduced such as being upside down. Be aware of the following points:

- To protect the Achilles' tendon, try to keep in positions where you can move your feet quickly, in case your partner slides off "the bench" and falls onto your heels.
- if you find the weight of your partner too much, simply roll down to the side and take up another position.
- Knee-pads, blankets or mats are especially useful here.

Photo 42: Heike Stiller and Keriac in "Mother Earth"

Exploring the bench: testing and dosing of weight
1. A is on all fours in the bench position.
2. B places hands onto the bench and tests out possible ways of giving and dosing weight.
3. B places hands onto the pelvic area or upper back and carefully increase the amount of weight. A becomes more active in support. How much weight can your partner accept? When and where does it become uncomfortable?

Photo 43

Balancing on the bench
1. A is on all fours in the bench position. Make sure the back is not sagging and the neck remains loose.
2. B lies with the back onto A, balances and rolls off. Use another person as helper.

Photo 44

Camel riding
1. A is in the bench position. B sits on the sacrum.
2. B sits upright and shoulders directly above A's pelvis.

3. A moves B, by sinking in the hips, rocking, rotating......
Variation: with feet on the sacrum, B stands up, the bench becoming a roman chariot.

Rolling under the bench
1. A is on all fours in the bench position.
2. B lies with the belly across the back of A.
3. With one hand on the floor for support, B slides the other arm underneath and through the bench, rolling on the shoulders under A. A is active and helps the slow slide by leaning in the opposite direction to the weight flow of B. B's legs stretch out, counterbalancing the weight of the torso.
4. It is recommended to change the roles quite often in this exercise in order to protect the knees. The dancers should maintain contact.

Photo 45

Rolling up the back
1. A sits, knees on the floor and leans forwards, placing the hands forward as support.
2. B lies across A's back (This is normally very relaxing for A!)

Photo 46

3. B, using the pelvis and torso, starts to roll up towards A's shoulders. This is normally like walking up a downwards escalator. A can help/hinder the process by adjusting the back's angle.

Headstand into roll
1. A is in the bench position
2. B goes into a headstand next to A, finds a point of contact between both backs, and slowly rolls backwards over A.

Variation: hand-stand instead of head-stand.

Photo 47

Giving impulses through arching your back
1. A is in the bench position.
2. B lies across the bench and A gives upward impetus through quite strong arching of the back.
3. B uses this momentum to move away and off the bench.

Rolling over the side of the bench
1. A is in the bench position.
2. B runs into a roll over A, weight evenly spread through shoulders and pelvis.

b) The back as a table.

Your partner stands, knees bent and leaning forward, using the hands on thighs as support and makes the back into a "table". It is useful not to use the arms as support however, letting them simply hang to the side, making them available for any consequent movement, remaining alert and flexible . Further tips for safety:

- Head and neck: do not bend it backwards but use it as support for your partner.
- Knees : let the weight travel down through your bones, not the muscles.
- Do not concentrate weight onto the table's spine or kidneys. - be careful not to push or pull the table.

Photo 48: Steve Paxton and Nancy Stark Smith, First ReUnion tour, 1975, Natural Dance Studio, Oakland, CA (Photo: Edmund Shea)

Exploring the table
1. A takes up the table position.
2. B places hands onto the pelvic area or upper back.
3. B slowly increases the amount of weight into the hands. A becomes more active in support.

Having the hands placed on the pelvis and shoulders is better for the giving and taking of weight. The weight of your partner can be guided over the arms and legs towards the floor (presuming the active participation of your partner in the fall!). Stop these exercises at the first sign of back pain.

Sliding off the table.
1. A sits on the table.
2. A slowly glides off. Explore ways and directions to slide off.

Rolling over the table.
1. A gets into a low table position, with hands on thighs as support.
2. B rolls over A, weight evenly spread through all shoulders and pelvis.

c) Trying out other surfaces.

All parts of our body can give and take weight. Play around with this idea - be creative!

Photo 49: Nancy Stark Smith and Curt Siddall, San Francisco Museum of Modern Art, ReUnion, 1976
(Photo: Rhoda Elend)

Sitting on shoulders.
1. A crouches down on the floor and B sits and balances on one shoulder.
2. A carries B forward slightly by leaning and lifting to the front.

Photo 50

2.3.2 Sloughing

We often get into positions when giving weight, where your partners body offers surfaces to lean and slide off from. All sides and surfaces of the body can be used.

Photo 51: N. Stark Smith and D. Lepkoff, Riverside Studios, London
On tour with "Free-lance", 1981
(Photo: Chris Harris)

Leaning on and casting off
1. A stands behind B. B leans against A
2. B slides slowly down A towards the floor.
3. During this slide, A presses B's pelvis towards the heels, with B ending in a crouching position.
4. A holds B's head and guides it gently towards the floor, sliding along the ground.

Photo 52

2.3.3 Body-Surfing

Taking weight should not be a rigid and inert affair, on the contrary: if we take weight and continue to roll, the weight feels much lighter and the rolling adds momentum to the ensuing shared movement.

2.3.4 Rolling with a partner

This section looks at how we can use our body as a kind of surfboard and find ways of balancing on a rolling partner. The skill is to maintain a shifting point of contact while rolling through the use of light and relaxed movement. As always, the roles of wave and surfer are exchanged: from riding on top to a rolling support. Certain parts of the body cannot take too much weight (knees, elbows, genitals, etc.) so please avoid giving your full weight into these areas. Use the floor to brace yourself allowing a more precise dosage of weight.

Belly to belly

Here we look at the possibilities of taking weight while lying, a controlled giving of weight and the different weight bearing capabilities of the various body parts.

1. A lies with the back on the floor.
2. B lies across A, gently giving more weight into the contact surface. Be aware of the physical and emotional sensations.
3. B rolls carefully towards A's feet, reducing the amount of weight around the partners pelvis, knees and ankles.
4. B rolls back towards the middle and continues up towards the head. Never place weight onto the head or neck. Find a light contact in this area.
5. B rolls back towards the middle, rests and listens to the body.

Taking your partner for a roll.

1. A lies on the floor, face up. B lies across A, belly to belly.

Photo 53

2. A rolls in a straight line, letting B ride (surf) across and slide onto the floor. B can experiment with different muscle tone; ranging from a sack of potatoes to stiff as a plank.

Rolling through the room.
1. A lies on the floor, face up. B lies across A, belly to belly.
2. A begins to roll and B surfs on top. The dancers now find ways to continue to surf with each other around the room with a fluid trading of roles.
3. Try to surf from different positions. Sideways, belly down, feet first.....

Further suggestions: from rolling to sitting to standing.
(The one on top is less active, but still maintains a certain muscle tone. The partner underneath (the wave) is active: when both are on the floor, the wave has to be quick not to lose the point of contact. If the one on top is loose in the hips, it is easier for the wave to move. When the wave is face down, it becomes a lot easier to move if the knees are pulled up towards the centre.)

Questions:
- Do I prefer the role of the wave or the surfer?
- Did I trust my partner not to hurt me?
- Did I make myself clear enough when there was too much weight? - Can I refuse someone and say NO?
- Do I feel too responsible for my partner sometimes?
- Is there a difference between dancing with a man and dancing with a woman?

2.4 Balance and counterbalance ───────────────

"To have the chance to live in the moment, to be absolutely present, listening to physical messages, allows us to find a playful, spontaneous, responsible and creative pathway - alone, pairs, or small groups. This path can also become a tightrope walk ; a balance between daring to take risks and remaining within your personal borders."[89]

Dieter Heitkamp

2.4.1 Balance

1. B lies on the ground and keeping the knees relaxed, stretches the legs into the air.
2. A leans/sits on the B's feet. A game of giving and taking weight begins....

Photo 54

2.4.2 Counterbalance: weight falls in or out

This is normally done in duets. Two people give weight to each other, support and control the balance. This can be done with arms or other parts of the body. There are two ways to counterbalance- away from and towards centre.

a) Leaning away from your partner.
1. Stand opposite your partner and hold hands.
2. Shake out shoulders, arms, wrists, making sure they are loose and relaxed.
3. Lean back slowly, feeling the pull in your arms. Shift your weight around slowly, all the time sensing your partners reactions.

b) Giving weight to your partner
1. Stand opposite your partner and place the palms of your hands together.(pat-a-cake!)

Photo 55: Keriac with students in Tübingen, Germany, 1981 (Photo: Bodo Zoege)

2. Lean in towards your partner. let the "push" come from your mass, not your muscles.

In both cases, a fine balance is needed. Without the other person you would fall down. An interesting game with small, slow shifts of weight occurs, without anyone taking the dominating role, as the balance is only present through co-operation and consideration.

Pressing against hands and improvising

1. A stands and presses sideways against a hand of B, who is sitting on the floor.
2. Through this pressure, a dynamic twist or turn can be felt, leading B into movement. Don't let B's feet touch the floor!

Photo 56

Questions:
- Can I give my whole weight, without losing a sense of my centre?
- What happens when my partner gives weight?
- can we find a mutual balance through co-operation?

2.5 Upside down: where is up? _____

"In contact improvisation we can depend on only three things: (1) one's self, (2) that the force of gravity works continually in one direction, down, and (3) that the floor supports our weight. It is a difficult task to say goodbye to that level line that we are unconsciously oriented to twenty-four hours of the day, the horizon."[90]

Curt Siddall

Photo 57: Scott Wells and Sean Seward
(Photo: Chryssa Novardy)

Lying upside down on your partner
1. Stand opposite your partner
2. Your partner bows down towards you. You lie over your partners back, head first. Your partner stands up slowly and carries you, upside down.
3. To put you down, your partner bends forward again.
Variation: lie across your partners back.

Photo 58

Shoulder stand with a partner
1. A stands in front of B, one leg in front of the other, knees bent.
2. A using hands as support, places a shoulder onto B's thigh.

3. A rolls up into a shoulder stand. B supports A by holding around the torso.

Photo 59

Hand-stand
The momentum for the hand-stand should not come from swinging the arms or legs but from a tilting of the pelvis, lifting it into the air, finally followed by a upwards stretching of the legs.

Helpful tips:
- arms are stretched and press into the floor.
- keep the neck long and head hanging, not flexed backwards.
- bend in the hips when coming down, landing softly on your feet.

1. Hands and fingers as suction pads
1. Warm up your hands by pressing and rolling them together.
2. One hand presses against the floor, the other points towards the ceiling. Feel the vertical connection between earth and sky.
3. Move around the room, pressing your hands onto the floor like the suckers of an octopus.
4. Keep increasing the weight in your hands and swing your legs off the floor.

2. Hand-stand against a partner.

1. Your partner does a hand-stand in front of you.
2. As a safety measure, hold your hands in front of you in case your partner kicks you in face.
3. Do not take a hold of your partner, but just prevent a tipping forward with a light support.
4. You can give your partner a gentle push back to help them get back to standing.

Photo 60

3. Hand-stand and lift

1. Do a hand-stand in front of your partner.
2. Your partner takes a firm and decisive grip around your hips and lifts. Make sure your arms are hanging down and ready to take weight.
3. Your partner gently lowers you down until your hands are on the floor and you can come out of the hand-stand by yourself.

Further suggestions: Your partner can carry you around the room for a short while.

Photo 61

4. Hand-stand and sitting on shoulder.

1. Do a hand-stand in front of your partner.
2. Put the back of your knees onto your partners shoulders and cross your legs around the neck of your partner. Bring your head up towards your partners.

139

3. Your partner can make it easier for you by stretching the lower arm out and letting you use them as levers.
4. As soon as you're sitting on your partners shoulders, uncross your legs and slide carefully down the side.

Photo 62

5. Back lift and roll-over

1. Stand back to back with your partner,
2. By bending your knees and sliding down your partners back, lean forward slightly and take your partner onto your back into a balanced position. Your partner remains quite relaxed at this point.
3. Your partner stretches arms over the head. You lean forward more, straightening your knees slightly. Make sure your partners hands are on the floor, directly under the shoulders.
4. Your partner now lifts first one knee then the other towards the chest.

Photo 63

5. As soon as you feel your partners weight is forward, help by straightening the knees a little more and give momentum to your partners swing to standing.
6. Both crouch down and look at each other!

Variation:
falling backwards from a hand-stand.
This variation should be done with a third person as spotter, holding onto the pelvis and preventing the person doing the hand-stand from falling onto their neck.

Photo 64

6. Into a duet from a hand-stand.
1. A and B are dueting
2. C tries to find a way in by doing a handstand.

Questions:
- When was the last time I did a hand-stand?
- Did I land safely?
- How does it feel being upside down?
- How do I behave when I am afraid? Do I express my fears?

2.6 Leaping and catching

"There is a state where mind and body are synchronised and balanced. Then there are no mental blocks and no physical blocks either..."[91]

Barbara Dilley

When we jump into the air, we are affected by two outside forces only; centripetal force and gravity. Our centre of gravity always describes an arc as when we throw a ball up into the air. We find at the topmost point of our jump the moment of least velocity. - just before our body starts to fall towards the floor. The scientific explanation; minimal velocity minimal momentum (momentum mass x velocity). The apex of the jump therefore is the best moment to catch someone. If we follow the direction of the jump before catching, it ends up smooth, flowing and astoundingly light. Please observe the following while catching:

- It is useful for the hands to be held in front of the body and ready to catch.
- Do not carry but guide the weight back down towards the floor. Support the movement by using your hands on your partners hips.
- Do not stiffen up, move with your partners movement and find a way into a duet.
- No crashing!

2.6.1 Leaps onto the back
Exploring ways to jump onto your partners back.
1. Your partner takes up the table position.
2. Place one hand onto the sacrum and the other hand onto the shoulder of your partner.
3. Jump (with care) onto your partners back

Variation: try the jumps with only one hand on your partners shoulder.

Jumping up
1. Your partner leans forward, knees bent, hands on knees.
2. Jump on to your partners back from behind or the side, turn, squirm, slide playfully around, glide to the floor..... jump on again......

Jumping on a table
1. From behind
a) Jumping past
b) Jump onto the sacrum of your partner and stand up.

142

c) Land with your lower legs and kneel.

Photo 65

2. From the side
a) Jump over
b) Turn to the side and slide down one leg
c) Forwards with your head down. Your torso is in contact with the lower back of your partner.

Photo 66

The roaming table
1. Your partner is a table. Jump onto it.
2. Let the table roam around the room.
3. Both sink to the floor.

2.6.2 Forward leaps

Preparatory exercise - leaping in space
Everyone jumps around the room - important: leap and turn 180 degrees, landing on both feet and look to the front. Allow the arms to fly up with the jump and let them fall down by themselves.

Supporting the hips while jumping

1. Bounce up and down like a tennis ball; knees and hips are loose.
2. Your partner holds the sides of your pelvis and in rhythm with your bounce, presses you down, increasing the rate of descent.
3. Swap roles often.
4. Rest by walking around the room and sense your feet!

Further suggestions: Bounce around the room with your partner.

Photo 67

Hands together and jump

1. Your partner stretches out the lower arms, palms up.
2. Put your palms onto your partners and jump. Let the jump come from your pelvis, feel a line pulling you up as if by magic!

Further suggestions: You continue jumping and your partner moves and turns around the room.

Weight in hands and jump away

1. Stand opposite your partner and place hands on each other.
2. Lean in towards your partner, giving weight.
3. Press yourself away, letting the energy lead you into a jump.

Jumping towards your partner

1. The group forms a circle, starting running slowly and jumping on the spot, landing on both feet.
2. One or two catchers are in the middle of the circle. One by one, the group jumps onto the catchers. Sideways, forwards, backwards....
3. The catchers take the weight and guide the leaper to the floor. The catchers can take a few steps with their "catch" if they want.....

Variation. The jumper slides to the floor using the catcher as post.

Jumping and being caught and carried

1. A jumps onto B, who catches with a kind of bear hug. It is important to catch at the right moment- not too early, wait for the weight to be close to the centre.
2. B carries A through the room.

Photo 68

Jumping towards your partner leading to a contact duet

1. Jump towards your partner
2. Let the resulting movement duet lead to the beginning of a contact duet. Stop as soon as both partners feel the starting point of the duet 3. Your partner jumps at you and repeat.....

Jumping towards your partner and rolling

1. Stand ready to catch
2. Your partner jumps into your arms, and rolls horizontally in towards your centre. This brings both centres of gravity closer together and lessens the effort needed to carry.

Photo 69

145

Jumping into a group of 3
1. Three people stand close together in a straight line
2. Jump into the arms of this group by running towards them at an angle, turning away and leaping with one leg raised, rather like a high-jumper, and fly... The first catcher holds under your arms, the middle one holds your hips, the last your lower legs.

Photo 70

Tips and images for the leaper
- Gliding along a wall.
- Jumping through a tyre.
- Jump into the air outstretched and stay up there for a second. - Always maintain muscle tone.

Further suggestions:
- The catchers use the momentum of the person jumping to move before putting the jumper down
- Simultaneously with being caught, the jumper pulls the legs towards the centre, regain control and gaining momentum to continue moving forwards.

2.6.3 Shoulder leaps

Jumping onto a shoulder and sitting.

1. Run towards your partner from behind, place hands on both of your partners shoulders, and jump up and sit on a shoulder.
2. To guide you down, your partner sinks in the knees and melts into the floor. Support yourself as soon as your feet touch the floor. This can also lead into a contact duet of course!

146

Photo 71 *Photo 72*

Shoulder leap from the side

1. To prepare for this jump, first run towards your partner at an angle from behind, place hands on both of your partners shoulders, and jump up , turn round and continue into the space without landing on your partner.
2. For the actual jump: your partner watches for your approach and uses the direction of your momentum to take a few stabilising steps.

Questions:
- What happens exactly when we jump and catch each other?
- How can I use gravity for these kinds of movements? Where is momentum? - Do I really look for the easiest mutual pathways all the time?

2.7 Lift

"...being prepared to let go of what you know, for what you can learn...."[92]

Michael Linehan

Indicating lifts - "marking"
1. A short duet to warm up
2. Just by indicating your intentions, "try out" various lifts to your partner, look for new ways. Do not actually lift but "mark".

Front lifts
1. Stand in front of your partner, cross your arms over those of your partner and hold on to the hips.
2. Your partner leans forward slightly.
3. Jump up, pivoting with your hands and lie across your partners shoulder.

Photo 73 and 74

Shoulder lift
If your partner lies on you like a sack of potatoes, it feels like a dead weight and you need to use a lot of effort in carrying. If your partner on the other hand, has a good muscle tone, stretches the extremities away from centre, it becomes much easier to carry and to balance. Try it out and see!

Preparatory exercise

a) Standing X: stretch both your arms up and place your feet apart, double the width of your shoulders. Two diagonal lines are formed (left hand to right foot and vice versa).
b) Lying X: lie on the floor and form the X - shape.

Variation: a sideways X!

Lifting onto the shoulder

1. Stand opposite your partner and look into each other's eyes
2. Bend down, keeping your back straight and under your partners centre, and place your hand onto the inside of your partners calf.
3. Both of you sink towards the floor a little.
4. On your word "Go", your partner jumps and across the back of your shoulders while you stand up.
5. Hold your partners leg and pull it slightly towards you.
   Your partner keeps a good stretch throughout the body and balances on top.

Photo 75

Important:

- Take the weight only when there is mutual agreement with your partner and your partner understands your non-verbal signals.
- Only hold your partner by the calf. This gives your partner freedom of movement.
- If you are afraid while on your partners shoulders, collapse like a sack of potatoes, in towards your partner, bringing your centre of gravity and therefore stability to the centre.
- Lifts should always be done with lightness and ease, otherwise something is wrong. Stop trying for a while and come back to it later.

Leaning and lifting
1. Stand prepared to lift
2. Your partner turns away from you, lifts arms and leans back against your front.
3. Your partner lifts a leg. You lift by placing one arm under the leg and one arm under your partners waist.

Photo 76

Questions:
- Do I become insecure while dancing if I lose my orientation?
- Can I carry someone or don't I dare to?
- Is there a difference if I do these exercises with a man or a woman?

2.8 Flying - dancing in the air

"... connecting center to center gives an increased ability to feel, mold, play. We use the skeleton to support the weight, the muscles to guide: no straining, not too much energy, but rather just the right amount used precisely, cleanly, with relaxation."[93]

Michael Linehan

Photo 77

Flying in the air means being at the point in the jump when the gravitational pull is not yet taking effect and you achieve a feeling of weightlessness - the highest point of the jump. Similarly it happens during certain lifts when your partner guides your whole weight upwards and you are released from the chains of gravity for a few moments!

Preparatory exercise: a leaf in the wind
1. Dance around the room, imagining that you are a leaf being blown around the space, carried up and dropped down.....
2. Experiment with different wind speeds.
3. Dance with a partner - two leaves in the wind.

The baby catch
1. Supporting yourself with an arm around your partners neck, swing into the arms of your partner.
2. Your partner uses your momentum to carry you for a few steps.

Further suggestions: jump up into the baby catch and keep going with your swing. Use your legs to help swinging past your partner by pulling them in and stretching them out again in the direction of your movement. You are not simply a weight on your partners shoulders!

Flying to the side
1. Stand side by side with your partner.
2. By sinking in your knees, bring your weight under your partner, and lift to the side by pressing your leg outwards, letting your partner lean against it (the waist is the pivot point).

Further suggestions:
1. by alternating roles of lifter and leaper with every jump, a travelling zigzag line can be described in space.

Photo 78

2. Let this develop into a free improvisation where the dancers can try out all the various jumps and lifts.

Questions:
- Do I trust my partner? Do I give my partner a sense of trust?
- How do I handle my misgivings in these situations? Do I make myself clear enough?
- What do I enjoy about being in the air? What do I dislike?

Photo 78a

3 IMPROVISATION

"Contact improvisation is an expression of sensitivity in both the physical and emotional realms. It demands, above all, the ability to yield to the present moment. ....People, like all creatures, are fearful of things unfamiliar. Working in this form one develops an appreciation of the unexpected within the realm of improvising and, I have found, outside of it in everyday life."[94]

Curt Siddall

Improvising is perhaps another name for "playing": curiosity, aimless experimentation, discovery, openness. One may think it is easier to get lots of creative ideas when improvising in a form, void of structure under the motto " dance what you want". But it is mostly not the case. We are hesitant, restricted to habitual movement patterns or simply resort to showmanship. "Only through the setting of priorities" said *Steve Paxton,* "was it possible to experience contact improvisation's particular form of fascination". Teaching experience shows that freedom, new discoveries and distinct statements often come about within a clearly defined structure or *"score".*

There are many exercises in contact improvisation which address these areas of awareness- exercises in which improvisation plays the leading role, or at least, ends up in that role.

3.1 Improvisation – awareness and skills

Physical skills and awareness states are difficult to approach separately in improvisation, and that is why in the following section, the exercises are split into three categories: Space, Time, and dynamics and Movement sources

3.1.1 Space

"Space in mind, mind in body, body in space"[95]

Lee Worley

a) Experience of space in movement
Visual focus
1. Walk around the room. Focus on a spot on the wall.
2. Walk directly towards this focus point. Just before you get there, choose another place to focus upon......

Being led through space
1. Close your eyes
2. Let your partner lead you through the room by holding your hand or arm. If you feel safe with your eyes closed, go faster. It is interesting to run through the space together or make quick directional changes.

Dancing the space between your partners body.
1. Start a duet with your partner.
2. Guide your attention and your dance towards the space between your partners limbs. Between head and arms, between knee and chest. Dance in this space.

Always walk in the middle.
Three people walk constantly through the space. Each person tries to keep walking in-between the other two. According to the amount of spatial awareness, this space in-between can be closed or opened. The gate becomes an area full of energy, alive with different qualities. Try to be sensitive to the situation and allow yourself a sense of "space".

It is important not to become over-ambitious and plan strategies. It is a game of balance - an active creation of space in-between weighted with an instinctual sense of space. Normally this game is very energetic but can have slow phases as well. Bring the game to an end when the group has expended its energy and are content.

Try different variations in the way of walking:

- Like water flowing through a narrow ravine
- Flutter like a butterfly
- Vocalise while walking

b) Spatial areas & levels

Crawling across a circle

1. The group forms a large circle by lying on the floor. One by one, crawl, slide, creep across the circle to the other side. Avoid contact with the others if you can.
2. Keeping low, crawl around and over a partner.

Guiding weight into the floor

1. Stand with your back to a partner
2. Lean back and give weight
3. Your partner spirals your weight down towards the floor.
4. Change roles and after a few times, let it go into a contact duet.

Mac the Knife

1. Everyone walks randomly around the space
2. One person secretively takes on the role of "Mac the Knife"; slashing down the back of whoever comes into range with his hand. The victim melts into the floor and stands up again - transformed into another "Mac the Knife".

Swooning to the floor through visual contact.

1. The whole group walks around the space. As soon as two people look into each other's eyes, they "swoon" and melt into the floor.
2. Let this develop into a swooning when two people touch. Variations: embrace each other when coming into contact and sink to the floor together, jump and shout together with each meeting.

c) Spatial pathways

Finding paths

1. Start off by letting each individual walk through the space, then building groups of two, then three until eventually the whole group is walking together through the room.
2. Try out variations: walking, jogging, running, with the Dolphin-Wave (p. 77).

Figure of eight

1. Stand as far apart from your partner as you can.
2. Walk in a figure of eight, coming closest to your partner at the crossover point.

3. a) walk past and look at each other
   b) at the crossover point, jump up as if you are madly in love with your partner!
   c) at the crossover point, jump up and shout an astonished "Oh"!

Draw the paths
This exercise helps to clarify the spatial patterns created in your dance.
1. Improvise a little "solo". Afterwards, draw your pathway down on a large piece of paper.
2. Improvise and let a partner draw your pathway while you are dancing.

d) Spatial dimensions (expanse)
Distance game
1. Choose a partner
2. Move and dance freely around the room but keep an "eye" on your partner. Dance a duet, come close together, far apart, keep contact through space.

Questions:
- How far apart can we go before I lose a sense of contact with my partner?
- Is there less contact the further apart we are?
- Is my skin the outermost part of myself?
- Do I really "know" the space around me or do I just think I know?

3.1.2 Time and dynamics

"In the middle of everyday life, create a refuge of playfulness and fantasy. Let your desires, dreams, fears, aspirations show themselves. Do the impossible - at least a scornful try, incite delight in playful freedom - in the macabre, impertinent, strange. Cut reality down to size, even if it always has to have the last word."[96]

COMPAGNIA BUFFO

The experience of time and the dynamics of movement are closely interrelated. Most of the previous exercises can be tried out using the following variations:
   - Slow motion
   - Lagging behind then speeding up.

- Continual or erratic
- Pulsating, rhythmic, spasmodic

Fast contact
The basic idea: intentionally introduce more momentum and dynamic into the duet. But even when you are going quickly - keep contact!

Breathing and swinging in the group.
1. Four or five people hold you by your arms. on your exhalation, lean back into the group and on inhalation, dance into the room with a "pah!".
2. The whole group: everyone dances to the rhythm of their breath. Let occasional physical contact give impetus to movement - Touch and Go.

Giving an impulse
1. Begin a slow dance
2. Your partner gives you impulses for movement by placing hands on your body.
3. Let your partner try out various ways of giving these signals - Randomly, wilfully, abrupt etc.

Variations:
- your partner shouts out different parts of the body for you to take movement impulses from.
- Dance with your eyes closed.

Questions:
- Do I prefer slow, steady movement or fast and dynamic?
- What does it feel like when I try out these other unfamiliar qualities in my dancing?
- What happens when aggression or affection come into play during dancing?

3.1.3 Movement sources

"One has to have enough chaos inside to give birth to a dancing star."[97]
Friedrich Nietzsche

There are multitude of sources for movement. The next chapter works with the following selection:

a) The body itself

"Our bodies are dynamic entities. Our cells are reproducing, processing and dying constantly as we live (...) Change is constant throughout the life cycle of the body. Structure is our physical body: the bones, muscles, and other tissue which compromises our bodies. Structure is affected by our heredity and by our life experiences ... Posture is the way we live in our structure ..."[98]

Andrea Olsen

Dance to order
1. Improvise in the space
2. Your partner calls out parts of your body for you to dance from... head, feet, tongue, ear, etc.

b) Moods and characters

"...using personality as an element of movement beyond the notion of "personal moving style" was a new step from old pathways for many of us opening a new range of valuable possibilities"[99]

Curt Siddal

Dancing emotions

Every dancer embodies an emotion or a mood. Dances can arise as clear conflicts or contrasts between emotions. *Steve Paxton* comments: *"This brings us to the non-physical part of this dancing; the state of being or mind permitting mutual freedom with mutual reliance, the mind is kept empty of preconceptions and memories; it is in the present moments only, meditating on the potentials and on the easiest paths in the energy construct which are available to both dancers: it is a state of abandon; trust in the self and in each other must be total. The ability to help each other and one's self must be ever ready: through constant movement one pursues mutual ease in constant mutual change. The dancer's weight is only his to give; not to possess."*[100]

c) Repetition, mirroring and alternation

"The question is how wise can an individual be in their dealings with forms which surround them? How much freedom can be found within form? How much freedom can Bach find in a canon? Bach found an enormous freedom in the strictest of forms..."[101]

Steve Paxton

1. Repetition
African dance (with music)
1. Find a movement, while listening to drumming, which reminds you of African dance.
2. Let the other members of the group copy your movement

Repetitive movement in contact.
1. Find a short movement sequence which can be repeated
2. Dance a contact duet and integrate this movement repetition into it.

Group improvisation:
Freeze ..... One. Two. Three.
- Everybody dances in the room.
- Anyone is allowed to call out at any moment, "Freeze!"
- Everybody freezes and holds the position they were in.
- After a call of "One. Two. Three", start moving again........

Group improvisation:
Video recorder.
1. Everybody dances in the room.
2. Anyone is allowed to call out at any moment the following video operating instructions:

- Play   (continue dancing)
- Pause   (freeze)
- Fast forward   (speed up your movement)
- Rewind   (reverse your movement)
- Fast rewind   (reverse even quicker)
- Slow motion   (slow down your movement)

2. Mirroring
Movement mirror
There are many possibilities open working with mirroring; copy the complete movement or only a specific part of the body ....

Mirroring with variations:
1. Stand opposite your partner. move in a way that your partner can copy you.

2. Variation: your partner copies your movement but makes slight changes. After changes roles, decide which variations can be used and which not. The following list of variations may be useful as starting points:

Size	Direction of walk
Speed	Spatial levels
Rhythm	Repetition
Dynamic	Changing the order of movement
Bodily orientation	Body parts
Spatial orientation	Adding material
Walking away	Excluding material

b) Mirror as reflection and feedback - The Witness
"...... the quiet slumber of the savagery in all joints..... they anchor themselves, turn, circle. Tired is the warrior..... head on the floor, legs in the air, the breeze - the world, it hurts sometimes..... shielding my body - stop! Looking hands and feeling fingers; the world and itself are lying in wait..."[102]

Lisa Sterr, after a dance as the witness

Development of an inner "authentic" movement.

1. Your partner goes into the middle of the space, eyes closed and starts a 30 minute improvisation.

Photo 79: (Photo: Archiv Moving Arts)

160

2. Your are the witness to this dance. Watch intently, take part in the dance process. You are also responsible for making sure that your partner is safe - doesn't hit the walls, crash into other people etc.
3. After the 30 minutes, both of you take a large piece of paper and draw a picture together - in silence. (The witness can dance her answers as well!)
4. Afterwards, give each other feedback about the dance and the picture.

Watch a duet and give feedback
1. Form groups of three. One sits to the side and is the observer of the duet.
2. After the duet has come to an end, the observer describes feelings and impressions experienced during the duet; were there different phases to be seen in the duet? Were both dancers equally involved? What were the qualities in this duet? What kind of pictures, emotions were invoked?

Variation: record the duet on video and watch it together.

3. Alternation
The "odd one out"
Form groups of three, a couple and the odd one out. The odd ones out dance through the space and look, through arm contact, to interrupt a duet and form a new one, leaving someone else the odd one out.

Copy and alter movement

1. The group forms a large circle.
2. One after another, make up a short movement sequence.
3. The rest of the group copies the movement but changes an aspect of it: rhythm, direction, dynamic, speed, intensity, etc. (See "mirroring" list above.)

d) Objects
"Our mind shifts its attention from object to object in erratic and irreverent ways. We can move from thought to feeling to imagination to remembering to sound to thought to taste to vision to thought ... the less

we control and inhibit this movement and the more we watch and listen, the freer our minds are to play with this vast assortment"[103]

Ruth Zaporah

Blanket Dance
Discover what you can do with a blanket!
1. Improvise around the space with a blanket as your partner.
2. Come into a contact duet with someone else, two dancers, two blankets.
3. Gradually abandon the blankets.

Installation
1. Split the group into threes and fours
2. Each group makes an installation with what ever objects are to be found in the space. Keep silent while making your objet d'art.
3. When finished, explore the object with movement, touch......

Questions:
- What kind of forms inspire what kind of movement?
- What images does the installation provoke? Memories?
- How do I transfer these feelings into movement?

e) Music
"Contact improvisation.... journeying with one or two partners..... moment to moment, a mutual creation of images and moods... with a smooth flowing in and out"[104]

Viki, after a contact workshop

In general, no music is used during contact improvisation, keeping an undivided attention on the physical process of the dance, letting that be the sole stimulus for movement - and not music. On the other hand, music can be an aid to getting people "going" with its provocation of images, emotions, dynamic etc.

Which kind of music creates which kind of movement?
1. Play short pieces (approx. 4 minutes) of different styles of music one after another. For example Chopin etudes, techno, waltzes, New Age music, African drumming, operetta...

2. Consider the following questions when improvising to the music: where in my body is this music located? What kind of movement do I want to do? what is my movement like when I don't like the music?

f) Focus on various scores

"I especially enjoyed the one where we danced with outward visual focus and then without focus. The change in spatial perception and interaction was amazing."[105]

Ray Chung

New sources for movement can be found by guiding your attention to different aspects of the dancing process on hand. A few ideas:

Twisting around each other
1. Lean back to back with your partner.
2. Your task is simply to keeping turning around your partner.

Photo 80

Sacral combat
1. Lean against your partner with the sacrum as contact point.
2. Give weight into the point of contact.
3. Try to push your partner away from you. Playfully!

Open and close like a flower
1. Lean against your partner with the sacrum as contact point.
2. Give weight into the point of contact.
3. Make some opening and closing movements: bend in the hips, torso comes forward and down; open up again - like a flower

Further suggestions: start a duet and integrate these opening and closing movements. This can lead to a very interesting dance!

Amiable non-co-operation
1. Dance a duet
2. Your partner is the leader and gives clear physical signs as to direction, level, dynamic etc.
3. Don't listen! Purposely go against the suggestions of your partner and promote your own ideas.

Applying impulsive pressure
Task: what level of pressure is too much? Too little? Comfortable?
1. Stand opposite your partner.
2. Push your partner somewhere on the body, giving your partner an impulse to move with.
3. Your partner says "Too much" or "Too little" - find the right amount.
4. Changes roles

Questions:
- What inspires me to move? Which sources? Which sources are unfamiliar? - What kind of movement habits can I see in others? What are my movement habits?
- Do I accept feedback? Can I take positive feedback?
- How does music affect me? And silence?
- What changes when I dance with my eyes closed? Or in front of people?
- How do I move in front of an audience? (not for an audience.)

3.2 Organisational forms of improvisation _____

3.2.1 Jams

An especially interesting form of collective dancing, which is not to be found in ballet or modern dance, found inclusion very early on in contact improvisation: the Jam. A group of people meet and dance together - without a teacher or any kind of leadership. Contact Jams are about exchange, mutual learning process and enjoyment. A non-hierarchical common relationship, in contrast to normal dance classes where someone passes on his or her knowledge or skills.

Many cities have regular jams (see address list in the appendix), if there isn't one near you - arrange one! A space to dance in, inside or outside, is always possible to find. A jam is a wonderful opportunity to meet other contact dancers, new playmates!

Photo 81: Bruno Stefanonie, Ka Rustler, Wolfgang Graf, Kurt Koegel
(Photo: Photozelle, s/w Labor, c/o Gisela Dilchert)

3.2.2 Round Robin

This form is used to ensure a flowing exchange of partners in a jam. One dance begins - ends - a new one starts. Who dances when and with whom is left open. Sometimes more than two dancers are in the middle at the same time.

1. Everybody sits or stands in a large circle.
2. One person (A) dances into the circle.
3. Eventually, another person (B) joins in the dance with A.
4. After a while either A or B leave and C enters the dance or C enters the duet and replaces A or B........ad infinitum........

Photo 82

The participants learn to let the dance find its own beginning and end. Curt Siddall writes: *"As the participants circle around the space a dynamic environment is created; in response to this environment, the dancers allow certain beginnings to occur. Intention and forcefulness have nothing to do with all of this.. the dance is ever changing, never the same. A series of events takes place as uninterrupted, pure transition from a beginning to an end. Working with contact improvisation is discovering how it feels to let this transition take place organically. In each individual duet it becomes apparent when an ending needs to happen. These dancers are obligated by the form to let these endings happen."*[106]

Everyone is active in the "round robin". There are no spectators. The circle protects and energises. Also it is interesting that the decision to go into the circle comes not from a "head" decision but from the belly. Literally, from the inner organs; the intestinal fall to the centre - the bones have no choice but to follow....

C TEACHING CONTACT IMPROVISATION

"Non-verbal communication is an important area in contact improvisation: a finely tuned ability to differentiate kinds of touch and the ability to read body language are necessary skills. Students have to be able to communicate their intentions non-verbally and learn to perceive and transfer all kinds of information in this way."[107]

Keriac

1 WHAT AM I TEACHING?

The development of physical skills and the sensitivity towards certain mind states are important factors in learning contact improvisation. But there is a danger in overemphasising these things. We should remind ourselves that these abilities are there to help us to feel at ease in particular areas of experience which we may face during dancing. The substance of contact is these experiences not the techniques used to get there. It is about the moon and not the finger pointing at it. It is important that the participants register their growing acceptance of disorientation. They should become aware of their body's organisational ability to "look after itself". Notice the greater trust in themselves and their partners and their enhanced ability to recognise what altering situation need. Students concentrate too often on perfecting a skill, a lift, a jump and something more important passes them by, as Randy Warshaw notes: " it's the orientation towards a higher and higher refinement that runs the risk of distracting students from the opportunities for a more personal exchange with their partner. the subtleties of any given moment can so easily be buried beneath the execution of that next move."

How and what is taught?

Self - awareness through playful improvisation

It is very important to have a deep inner integration of the principles of improvisation. It can lead to exhilarating moments where you abandon having to know everything beforehand, abandon aims and ambitions, abandon rushing from one place to the next, and simply sense yourself being in a moment of pleasurable lingering in the here-and-now. Giving yourself completely to the moment, open to inspiration - improvising - can give you trust in the "dynamic of the temporary". Fear, of the uncontrolled, metamorphoses into a curiosity - regardless of it being comfortable or not.

Learning by doing
Because contact improvisation isn't based on a rigid technique or virtuosity, there can be no real rights or wrongs in moving. Learning comes more from a intimate study of the consequences of movement : if I do that, then this happens, but if I change it slightly, something else happens. It is about giving opportunity, leaving things open and improvised. The only knowledge passed on verbally are safety tips on how to avoid injury.

Learning is a process of alternation
The teacher makes things possible and could be called the energy channel. If the students do not bring energy, the teacher cannot channel - nothing happens and we all go home.

Value the diversity of perception and approaches in the class
One is often surprised to see a greatly varying range of awareness states and sensitivity in the participants. Each person has a unique existential reality and individual pace which is to be respected. That is why nothing should be forced while teaching; the exercises should be presented more as suggestions and invitations to explore.

The student is the teacher
Beginners learn to see a dual role for themselves: student and teacher. This "implantation" as Keriac describes it, is passed on through the generations of contact dancers ensuring contact's continuance as the form of non-form. The dance is where the teaching happens. The teacher points the way.

Avoid conceit
Teaching a workshop is not an opportunity for you to polish and repair your ego.....open criticism and contradictory participants are no reason

for you to become defensive and closed either. The participants are at the forefront of any "class" - contact improvisation is a communicative movement form, accepting all emotional information into the dance. Don't block this emotional energy of the participants, use it, transform it into dance. Of course, the leader of the workshop always has the right to decide about the constellation of the group and need not tolerate the inexhaustible squabbler.

Photo 83

2 How do I structure my classes?

Decide upon a theme and find your own exercises
There are two possibilities when teaching:
1. Decide upon a theme for the class / workshop beforehand and choose suitable exercises (or develop your own exercises, it's easier you than you might think!)
2. Decide upon a theme for the class / workshop beforehand and choose one exercise to warm up with and serve as a "starter". Leave the rest of the class up to your intuition and sense of the group energy. Follow the flow. This should only be attempted after you have experience in teaching though, otherwise whenever the energy stagnates and you can't think of what to do next, you'll appear unprepared and might give the participants a feeling of insecurity.

Some suggestions for teaching
- Start with exercises for self-awareness then into awareness of a partner
- Practise solo skills and awareness states. Follow that with partner work then the whole group together.
- Make sure the roles within the partner exercises are in flux and try to encourage the swapping around of partners as well.
- Create "performance spaces" occasionally; half of the group are in the middle dueting while the others sit around the side and watch. Short solos, duets........
- Feedback is important. Make sure you have enough time to talk, watch, paint, write......
- Don't keep rigidly to exercises - at the beginning of contact improvisation there were none! Exercises are a means to an end - not more and not less.

3 THREE DIFFERENT CLASS STRUCTURES

The following structures are for classes of approximately two hours and have been used in classes with adult beginners. Improvisation was used throughout as the fundamental method.

Naturally, each contact teacher chooses methods, structures, etc. to suit their own abilities and preferences. The following structures, dealing with the three spatial levels; low, middle and high, serve only as examples.

Structure 1 _____

Contact improvisation - Low

The central theme in the first part of this class is getting to know the floor, sensitising the body surfaces and generally experiencing oneself as weight. The second part uses this experience with a partner.

Arriving:
- Each member of the group walks around the space and remembers in detail the pathway they travelled to get to the space where they find themselves.
- Sit in a circle and a short personal introduction from everybody.

Warming up:
- Rocking the feet (Bartenieff-exercise) (p.75)
- Moving the legs in all directions. (p.75)
- Round like a ball. (p.106)

Sensing:
- Sensing the connections of the various parts of the body (p.77)
- Sacrum to sacrum (p.116)

Introduce the theme (sit in a circle) with the following exercises:
- Rolling along the longitudinal axis (p.107)
- Body surfing (p.132)
- Improvisation - from the floor to standing

Warm down:
- Everyone finds a place in the room and spends a few minutes in silence - sitting, lying, standing...
- Feedback: sit in a circle and talk about the last two hours. Helpful question:" how do I feel right now?"

Photo 84

Structure 2

Contact improvisation - Middle

The themes of this class include weight carrying abilities of the various body surfaces, giving your whole weight and mutual support.

Arriving in the space:
- Small dance (p.101)

Warming up:
- Mobilising the joints (p.74)
- The dolphin wave (p.76)
- Diagonal Stretching in threes (p.80)

Sensing:
- Sensing and expanding the breath (p.82)
- The sacrum game (p.121) followed by free improvisation.

Introduce the theme and the following exercises:
- Crawling over your partner (p.120)
- Exploring the bench: testing and dosing of weight (p.127)

- Camel riding (p.127)
- Rolling under the bench - into free improvisation

Photo 85

Warm down:
- Breath and voice (p.82)
- Feedback

Photo 86:
(Photo: Claudia Diebold)

Structure 3

Contact improvisation - High

The themes : learning to appreciate disorientation, falling and moving off centre, jumping and lifting.

Arrival:
- Various stretching exercises
- Moving down towards the floor (p.110)
- Falling and standing up (p.111)
- Swing and jump (p.114)

Sensing:
- Leaning on and casting off (p.132)
- Sacral combat (p.163)
- Slow motion contact improvisation

Introduce the theme and the following exercises:
- Exploring the table (p.130)
- Jumping in the room (p.143)
- Jumping on the table (p.142)
- Marking lifts (p.148)
- Shoulder lifts (p.148)
- Round robin (p.165)

Warm down
- Massage and coming to standing (p.82)

Foto 87

4 STAGING AND PERFORMANCE

"Presence on stage is a thing of great beauty"[108]

Stephan St. Keuter

A stage is a very special place, usually full of alertness and presence. The spectators focus their attention into this area, directly influencing the performers. The stage is to be understood as any place where one or more people offer their work to an audience - formal stage settings or just in the middle of a circle. A stage is created in a class when watching participants in duets or solos; guest are invited to stage their work at the end of a workshop.

The stage is a "hot spot", a domain of reality, full of energy, immediacy, presence and, in a way, of nakedness. An alert onlooker senses immediately if a performer is vigilant and authentic and able to create a subtle channel of communication with the audience - or whether it is a simple narcissitic display, perhaps of virtuosity, but eventually leading to audience indifference.

There is always a special atmospheere created during a performance, an "energy cycle", as Keriac states, " between the actors and the spectators. This bond is broken with television, for example".

Where is the centre of the stage?
Walk slowly onto the stage. Find the strongest part of it, the part where you feel the most energy. Try different areas of the stage, sense its strength. When you have found your personal "hot spot", stay there for a while. All the other participants become spectators and take part in your search.

Further stage ideas:
- Practice entrances and exits
- Explore the difference beween looking into the audience and not looking.

D AREAS OF APPLICATION FOR CONTACT IMPROVISATION

Contact improvisation is mainly taught within the professional dance scene, adult education, in conjunction with sport education or for dance teachers. this section of the book deals with particular areas of application for contact improvisation.

1 CONTACT IMPROVISATION WITH THE DISABLED

"Dancing with disabled people taught me an enormous amount ... it can take us away from "beautiful forms" and "big, acrobatic movement" and show us to appreciate the little sensitive movements again. It brings us back to a modest, simple and sensitive state of mind and leads us to our essence: our heart"[109]

Adrian Olender

A few contact teachers work and dance intensively with the disabled. *Alito Alessi* for example co-founded "DanceAbility" with Karen Nelson creating impressive performances with disabled and non-disabled dancers. Nelson continues her mixed abilit work through her 'diverse Dance' project.

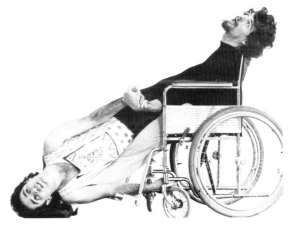

Photo 88: Contact-Duett with Alito Alessi & Emery Blackwell (Photo: Sean Poston, Archiv Moving Arts)

What follows here is a summary of an article by *Alice Lusterman*, "Structuring contact activities for children with learning disabilities that originally appeared in Contact Quarterly Magazine, Vol III No. 1, Fall 1977.

Such children show the following tendencies: easily distracted, unable to differentiate between relevant and non-relevant signals and stimuli, difficulties in concentration. Their short-term memory is often impaired, which makes it difficult to follow lessons at school as well as limiting physical dexterity. They have lack of control and are often hyperactive. A disturbance in their spatial or temporal orientation often results in disorganised or unco-ordinated movement activity. And they tend to have low esteem. Practical experience shows that a healing process can take place if children move together, respect themselves and others on a physical level and enjoy the feeling of physical bonding which is set free during physical contact.

This work can be split into the following six aspects:

1.1 Body image

Body image is formed through tactile and kinaesthetic sensations from outside stimuli such as touch or inner stimuli such as feedback from muscle activity. Information for body awareness is collected through strong motor activity, small movements and even when at rest. Children with learning disabilities have a disturbed body image. Physical sensations are not correctly registered or remembered and do not adjust to new situations. It appears necessary therefore that these children are offered structured repetitive exercises. The following have been found useful:

- Movement of individual body parts and finding new movement possibilities. We can start with arm or head movements followed up by back, chest, or hips.
- Experience the body as a whole: two children sit back to back with eyes closed. Keeping contact with each other through their backs, they rock from side to side, forwards and backwards, etc. The contact and the slow shifting of weight gives the children tactile information which brings them awareness of the body as a whole - themselves and their border with the rest of the world.

1.2 Postural alignment

Effecient postural alignment is achieved when the three big "weights" of our body - head, chest and pelvis - are balanced on top of each other so that the weight flows easily down the bones into the floor. Exercises:

- Each child curls up on the floor and forms a "snowball". One by one, the teacher slowly stretches them out and leads them to standing ; a snowman. Each body "weight" is a snowball stacked on top of each other. The unrolling helps to centre the weight on a central axis. When all children are standing, the snow can melt and they sink slowly to the floor. The teacher can then massage and rotate the childrens joints - head, shoulders, arms......
- The image of a thread or rope reaching up from the head to the ceiling, stretching out the spine is also very helpful.

1.3 Balance

To balance on one leg for example, the child has to concentrate and stop their typical uncontrolled movements.

- The children balance on different parts of their bodies - hands, feet, knees - and in the three spatial levels. They can curl up or stretch out to find their balance. It is important to find a large variety of movement so they can feel the connection with their daily lives. The fun involved in such movements is a strong motivating force for the children and promotes concentration and self-control.

1.4 Control of energy: tension and relaxation

If children can develop a better control over their excitement or physical tension, they can dose this energy output in a more suitable way. This makes their behaviour more efficient and satisfactory. It also helps to sustain their attention onto one activity. Through relaxation exercises, the children experience calmness, an easy energy output and a sense of themselves at rest. A useful exercise here is the "human bridge":

- Each child balances on one leg and touches another child with another body part. This balances melts slowly (or drops quickly) onto the floor. They both get up from the floor, come back together and roll over each other. This exercise helps to control energy and speed and brings a pleasure in kinaesthetic and tactile experience.

1.5 Organisation in time and space

Children with learning disabilities often lack a clear sense of spatial dimensions when they move. That's why it is so important for them to experience up and down movements in space, under or over a table, in and out of a circle.

- Moving around the room: rolling, crawling, running, jumping. Through the room like a snake, sliding on skates, turning like a propeller.
- The children move to drum music or songs. It is important to promote moving to their own sense of time, to get a feeling for their own rhythm (organisation of body in time is helped through rhythmic tasks).

1.6 Self - image

In order to have a positive self-image, it is essential to be able to make your own decisions. But not knowing a world of myriad individual choices, the children have no knowledge of choice. At the beginning of each session it is wise to have clearly structured exercises with definite tasks. This is necessary to control their own behavior. Another reason is that the children have a lack of body awareness, limiting their ability to use the complete movement vocabulary. Through development of self-control and self-confidence, they are more able to express themselves with free and selected movements. The opportunity to express themselves with a newly defined body language strengthens their self-image. In dance, the children can be "seen", they feel understood and learn to value themselves and what they do.

1.7 Moving with a partner

Contact can start on a very different level : visual contact with a partner. the children can sit in a circle, roll a tennis ball to someone and look into each other's eyes. Another exercise:

- Children sit opposite one another. they take the partner's head in their hands, move it carefully around and keep eye contact. Gradually the movement should become more precise; side to side, or backwards and forwards. Included in this exercise is the responsibilty for your partner and the necessary co-operation. If the children are well prepared through such exercises, basic elements of contact improvisation can be introduced: body surfaces, giving weight to a partner, offering support....

Conclusion: contact improvisation can help children to become more aware of their bodies, promoting a sense of well-being and greater trust. Being a partner in a group makes them more sensitive to the needs of other children, develops a co-operative readiness and a pleasure in mutual experience of physicality and mind states.

2. DANCE THERAPY:
THE CONTACT DUET AS A REFLECTION OF HUMAN RELATIONSHIPS AND COMMUNICATION

"Movement shows the biographic chronicle of a personality; the interplay between the present and past"[110]

Hilarion Petzold

A lot of contact dancers feel that through contact improvisation they gain insight into themselves, emotional maturity and are able to integrate the contact principles into their daily lives. It is possible to train both mental and physical flexibilty and strength. While dancing, we find ourselves in continual change, a flow which invites, even requires ones bodily, aesthetic, and mental concepts to change. Though contact improvisation was not developed with therapy in mind, nevertheless it often has a therapeutic effect. To be in contact with someone over a long period of time, to experience physical intimacy, to let your-self be touched, to give support are all healing processes.

A contact duet reflects many psychologically relevant aspects: intimacy, trust, hesitancy, borders, assertion, dependence, independence, co-operation, control, risk taking, letting go. The way of contact with another person depends to a certain extent on need. While doing contact improvisation, a very sensitive yet energy laden connection is made with the other person and simultaneously with one's self. In this way, contact improvisation brings deep down feelings closer to the surface and allows them to be experienced. They can become part of the movement. The focus stays with the physical activity however and does not drift away towards interpretation. It is about the physical sensation of moving, the joy and simplicity of one's own movement (which is often lost during a more formal dance training).

Through contact improvisation, many people have an increased sense of well-being and experience pleasure and security in groups. Sometimes students start crying or start talking about intimate details of their personal life, fears and anger arise, the need to be touched, in contact, to feel support and be able to give support. But the dance always continues and the energy, not so much the emotions, is given a free rein (usually, anyway!). Trust and support have the chance to grow, we can face new and strange situations. A mindfulness for the here-and-now, allow ourselves to be attentive and let our feelings come to the surface.

The contact dancers working in areas of therapy find their personal experience of contact spilling into their daily (working) lives. The question arises: in what way can contact improvisation benefit my clients?

Dance and Movement Therapy

Acknowledging the variety of directions in dance and movement therapy in Europe, the following section will draw upon the Integrative Dance and Movement Therapy, developed by Hilarion Petzold. To be healing liberating and preventative, she describes three distinctions:

- Task centred - functioning: recognising and influencing physical conditions such as breath, tension, power, coordination; self-confidence through awareness
- Conflict centred - exposing: bringing the hidden conflicts out of the shadows in to the light of consciousness and allowing integration.
- Experience centred - stimulating: encountering different qualities of experience, stimulating the task centred work towards a deeper and holistic experience and transfering the conflict centred work into a "body memory"

Movement therapy uses, as *Hilarion Petzold* describes," a whole range of partner exercises, imitation, synchronisation, mirroring of movement and movement sequences and empathic anticipation of movement sequences. Dancing together is especially emphasised in dance therapy. With increasing ability in "dancing together", the patients become more skilled in finding solutions in a social context, become more sympathetic - an increase in vitality, a healing." Trying to hold on to fixed patterning, old habits results in " the loss of vitality, an obstruction of inner movement..... a blocking of togetherness through movement, relationships, ties." The price is high this "security through fixation" as Petzold continues; " the loss of movement in a

182

social context and further into the real world is the loss of vitality because again: life is movement".

This has many parallels with contact improvisation. Contact brings valuable experiences, practical ideas and simply the joy of dance and "meeting through movement" to Dance Therapy. But perhaps most importantly this vital dance form should retain its anarchic freshness, not become institutionalised and included in a esoteric/spiritual shopping list. Contact as a reflection of human relationships and in others.

3 CONTACT IMPROVISATION IN DANCE EDUCATION: KERIACS "DANCING TOGETHER"

The following text was written by Keriac.

"I have made it my life's purpose to offer a safe space for dance artists to let their passion for dance burn brightly. Ever since my childhood, I have felt a strong drive to participate in creative projects that involved dance, theater and singing. At one point, I decided that this force driving me was neurotic need and not healthy. I tried to extinguish it, only to discover that I was trying to blow out a source of joy and a profoundly healing power - it was, in fact, my own identity and life-force. This taught me respect for the creative drive in myself and others. People often keep this aspect of themselves hidden, sometimes because of a lack of support in the family or in the wider culture. For myself and many people, art is not an activity kept for casual moments at the periphery of their lives, it is a flame burning at their core.

"Dancing Together" the Intensive Training Program for New Dance Performance which I lead in Europe and the USA, provides dancers with guidance, support and the opportunity to develop their creative potential of „Dancing Together" explore dance as an art form through a balanced program of dance technique, dance creation and performance. Taking place in San Francisco, USA and Stuttgart, Germany, this bi-cultural program has fostered the creative growth of students from countries around the globe, including Israel, Switzerland, Austria, France, Germany, Belgium, Japan, Holland, America and Rumania. English is spoken in the US classes, whereas German is the language used in Europe. Performance, the mode through which dance communication takes place, is the main goal of the program. This is a full-time program in which students train 6-8 hours per day for six months to two years. Classes are multi-level, with beginners and advanced students together in certain classes, and separate in others.

Men and woman from the ages of 21 to 65 have taken part during the last ten years of the program's history. This rich mixture provides a variety of models for learning as well as opportunity for peer coaching. An atmosphere is created in which each person can be accepted, and can accept themselves, as they now are. From that base, each can take the next appropriate step to their individual development.

Dance, as the oldest art, extends back to the time in human history when art, religion and healing were not separated, and when individual identity was not so emphasized as in today's western culture. People are gregarious. Just like our ancestors, the monkeys, we naturally gather in groups or tribes.

Our human nature is not fulfilled without this wider social dimension to our lives. At its essence, dance is a transcendental and communal activity. A large part of the pleasure of viewing dance performance is being a part of the collective body, the audience, with its infectious laughing, sighing, crying. We realize that we are not the only ones with these feelings. Through these shared moments, a common culture is built in a people. Our common cultural base supports a shared value system, and ultimately helps define the meaning of our lives.

My first years of Contact were in the context of community - about 150 people all learned this form around the same time. We all went to the same workshops and performances; we unquestioningly attended every contact intensive. It was the "in" thing to do - there was an exhilarating sense of excitement and adventure that swept through us. Many of us, myself included, had also learned about group process through our study with Anna Halprin. We became a sub-culture of the San Francisco alternative scene: an egalitarian, non-hierarchical, loving and warm, health-oriented social organism. I was proud to be a participant because it reflected my politics and the values I believed in. The dancing itself embodied the co-operative model I wanted for all my relationships. After years of rebelling against the mainstream, working as a lonesome pioneer in what some may have thought were weird experiments, I could at last identify with a dance group. I was a child of the 60's and Contact was my dance.

In "Dancing Together", my students' work in contact improvisation deepens their teamwork and supports a healthy group process. The playfulness of contact, with its experiences of touch and shared weight, lead to trusting relationships and greater group co-operation. This, paradoxically, allows each person more individual freedom. It gives the self confidence needed to explore a unique vision in the solo performance work that is also a major focus of the "Dancing Together" program.

Contact Improvisation is a form to which I can say "Yes!" it is an aesthetic worthy of my life-long exploration. In very practical terms, contact has become my physical discipline - a replacement for the ballet and modern dance technique that in my youth, I scorned as being rote learning "without soul". Contact has taught me body mastery through problem solving, not through learning steps. It has led me to a daily confrontation with those stern but liberating taskmasters, gravity and momentum. I have come to appreciate the quiet power of my skeleton and structure. I enjoy the precision of "effortless" movement - when only the necessary muscles work at the right moment in the flow, and all else is left at rest. The constant contact with floor and bodies, the sensuality, the daily releasing and massage work, all enrich my life with a feeling of unconditional love. This does wonders for my self-confidence and for my satisfaction in life!

I have taught weekly contact improvisation classes and countless weekend workshops continuously since 1979. My students have included children ages 7-10, seniors ages 70-88, blind people, teachers of adults and children, married couples and even patients who were victims of phobia. I have taught contact to a convention of radical psychiatrists, to communal family members of several San Francisco Communes, to doctors, engineers, and business executives as well as actors, professional dancers and sculptors. This experience has shown me that contact can be tailored to the needs of extremely diverse groups because its essence is universal. To me, contact is simultaneously profound and mundane, like breathing."

Keriac was introduced to contact improvisation through her dance partner, Charles Cambell. In 1977, she also began studying with Charles' teacher, Byron Brown, who was himself a student of Nita Little (ReUnion). He later co-founded the Mangrove Dance Collective.

In 1978, Keriac attended the summer intensive taught by members of the Bay Area Contact Coalition. Her other early contact improvisation teachers were Curt Siddall (Re Union) and John LeFan, also co-founders of Mangrove, and Nancy Stark Smith and Steve Paxton (both ReUnion). In 1979, with 10 other contact dancers, Keriac co-founded the Walkabout Dance Collective, who were an important source of her support and learning for the next several years. Over the past 20 years, Keriac has attended numerous contact improvisation jams and conferences in the USA and Europe, where she had the opportunity to exchange ideas and dancing with many American and European contact dancers. Keriac has taught contact improvisation continuously since 1979, and also credits her students for much of her own growth in this dance form.

4 CREATIVE PROCESS AND MEDITATION – TWO STREAMS (BY BARBARA DILLEY)

Five Eye Practices
Closed eyes: internal seeing; rest; refresh
Peripheral seeing: soft focus; seeing from the corner of the eyes
Internal eyes: seeing before naming
Looking between things: the space "between"; negative space
Direct looking: investigate; study; absorb
From : Naked Face, Barbara Dilley with the Mariposa Collective, 1996
A talk by Barbara Dilley
Naropa Arts Weekend
New York City
7th Nov. 1986

Introduction

I'm delighted to be here, and I'm very glad that all of you came to listen to this story. It is a story I haven't told for a while. When I came to New York last Monday from Colorado, I was reminded of leaving here years ago when I was a student of dance and a part of the contemporary art scene that was flourishing at the time. I lived here from 1960 until 1975. I studied dance and joined the Merce Cunningham Dance Company and became involved with the more experimental avant-garde work that came from the Judson Dance Theater. By the time I left in 1975, I had begun to choreograph and perform my own work. I was committed to the art of improvisation and was exploring how to teach it to others. Perhaps the training ground that was most provocative for me was the arena of the Grand Union, the arena of spontaneous improvisation.

I want to tell you about the mingling of two streams, two threads, that began to join and weave together. The first thread, or stream is the contemporary American dance improvisational form. I never learned it from anyone. It came to me by playing together with my dancing friends and by performing with them. The play would become the performance. The 60's was a time of play and music and altered states. It was a time of discoveries and investigations, the freedom to explore and experience our sense fields, our perceptions; looking at the boundaries, and talking about it together. As young artists, performing artists, we investigated the world around us. The improvisational work was the way we explored. We were looking at how we perceive, how our minds connect with sense perceptions of bodies in space, of sound affecting gesture, of being influenced by what was there.

In improvisation forms, we connect very clearly to the constant shifting that exists in our perceptions; as the mind travels along, attention lasts only so long in any particular area before it flips, jumps, dodges or darts in other directions. This awareness became the ground for spontaneous dance improvisation. Formal training in traditional dance forms is equally important in the evolution of this thread of improvisation. sometimes it is forgotten or not placed clearly in the pattern of development. We all had formal dance training. We did daily technique classes. We went to performances of all kinds. We performed, rehearsed and spent long nights hanging out with various choreographers while they figured out what they wanted to do.

4.1 Teachers

There were some strong teachers, mentors, around. I was very influenced by John Cage and his writing. "Silence" was published about 1960 just as I left college. It presented an approach to perceptual awareness that was authentic to me. "A Year from Monday" is an intriguing collection of stories and talks about his explorations with composition, indeterminacy and chance; all acknowledging this play and shiftiness of mind's attention.

I had the good fortune of working and studying with that master teacher and movement inventor Merce Cunningham. He is a most important and powerful part of my heritage. He definitely helped to create the definition of contemporary American Dance. He is part of the lineage of this stream. One very strong aspect of this time was what I call a "dialogue of artists." I feel that truly strong cultural growth occurs when there are artists talking and listening and watching and critiquing, sharing and struggling with their intimacies and perceptions and intelligence. That kind of environment is provocative, invigorating and it stimulates the evolution of creativity and expression. Another thread in this pattern as I perceive it is the work of Yvonne Rainer. The Grand Union, a group which evolved from Yvonne's work, was a collection of young, strong-minded and creative people who created a „dialogue of artists." In the Grand Union we tended to throw away conventions and dare to be ourselves. We would open the curtain and begin to perform. The heat got turned up and we just manifested. It was improvisational dance theater and it was a new form. Some parts of each night we performed were exceptional, some were ordinary and some were boring. It was in these events that I discovered what the edge meant - being pushed to it, wandering toward it and backing away, or just realizing I was there and ... here we go, over it. it was the familiar meeting the unfamiliar and it was a shock. It was a place unlike any been to before. Obviously it was located in reality but the question was "what reality?" There were unexpected forms, shifting one focus to another, from one frame of reference to another, very suddenly. This may sound familiar to you or it may not. It wasn't particularly familiar to me at the time but it became a place of creativity. It was at that place where the heat was up and you didn't know what was going on so you had to make it up. You did, and it worked, somehow, and you went on to the next gesture. That experience of making it up, on the spot, was the Grand Union.

However, in that experience of the Grand Union there was something disturbing. The world was constantly shifting and there wasn't much to hang on to. There was a psychic tremulation, a tenderness or awkwardness that was vague and disconcerting.

4.2 The Narope Institute

In 1974, I was invited to The Naropa Institute in Colorado. I didn't know anything about the place. A friend who helped to organize the events of that first summer invited me to teach. He had seen some of the work I was doing in New York. He said that it seemed very connected to what was happening at Naropa. That summer, I listened to the talks of the founder, the Vidyadhara, the Venerable Chogyam Trungpa, Rinpoche. I decided that I wanted to explore the meditation practice that he spoke about. I decided to sit down. The images of meditation in the Buddhist tradition captured my heart and my mind. Meditation is described by Trungpa, Rinpoche as taming the wild mind. Coming from the heat of those wild improvisations, I knew what he was talking about. The mind was definitely let loose in that arena of spontaneous performance. I had no idea of how to tame it. I wasn't even sure that I wanted to but there was this disconcerting bewilderment, and often a dull sense of pain.

This was the beginning of the second thread for me. And it brought together the contemporary American improvisational dance form with the great teachings of Buddhism. These were the two streams, two threads. One of the great images from the practice of meditation as it was taught at The Naropa Institute is "mingling the mind with space." In improvisational dance I felt that I was mingling the body with space. So these two activities were similar for me - the space in which the movement and the dance happens and the space out into which the thoughts and mind move. I was captivated by the image of connecting these two energies of mind awareness and body activity, together. It was the practice and study of meditation that showed the way.

Another description of meditation was to cultivate awareness. That word began to haunt me . . . awareness. Searching for awareness infused all the work I was attending to and it connected to my passion for teaching; developing awareness. It was fundamental. There was awareness of the mind and of the activities of mind, and of the rhythm of that activity. When I was improvising I wanted to express the rhythm of mind, the pulse, shift, gap. Not the content, but the shape, color, dimension, length - and the suddenness.

And perhaps the most powerful words that I heard from Trungpa, Rinpoche that first summer were "Non-aggressive Art." It was like a large bell was struck deep inside me. So much of what I felt about the art world at that time was filled with tinges of aggression, with competition and push. And because of this, I found myself hesitating in my journey as an artist.

4.3 Dharma Art

I was very excited by the image of Dharma Art as laid out by Trungpa, Rinpoche. "Dharma" means the truth, "the-way-it-is", the norm. It is completely refreshing. And what grew quite naturally from this was the sense of "art in everyday life." It is seductive and full of potential. It seems to offer the way to heal any sense of separation or schizophrenia that is an underlying pulse of the western art world.

Dharma Art Letter

In talking about Dharma Art here, we do not mean art which necessarily depicts Buddhist symbols or ideas - the wheel of life, the story of Gautama Buddha, etc.- but rather art which springs from a certain state of mind on the part of the artist. We can call this the meditative state: an attitude of directness and unself-consciousness in one's creative work.

The basic problem in artistic endeavour is the tendency to split the artist from the „audience", trying to send a message from one to the other. When this happens, art becomes exhibitionism: the person who gets some tremendous flash of inspiration, then rushes to „put it down on paper" to impress and excite others; or the very deliberate artist who strategizes each step of his work to produce certain effects on his viewers. No matter how well intentioned or how technically accomplished, these approaches inevitably become somehow clumsy and aggressive, toward others and toward oneself.

Chögyam Trungpa, Rinpoche (July 1974)

In „meditative" art, the artist embodies the viewer as well as the creator as he works. Vision is not separate from operation, and there is no fear of being clumsy or failing to achieve his aspiration: he simply makes his painting, poem, piece of music, whatever.

In this sense, a complete novice could pick up a brush and, with the right state of mind, produce a masterpiece. This is possible. But it is a very hit-and-miss approach. In art, as in life generally, we need to study our craft, develop our skills, and absorb the knowledge and insight passed down by tradition.

But whether we have the attitude of a student, who could still become more proficient in handling his materials, or the attitude of an accomplished master, when we are actually creating a work of art there is a sense of total confidence; our message is simply appreciating the nature of things as they are and expressing it without any struggle of thoughts and fears. We give up aggression, either toward ourselves - ourselves as the center of everything, that self is understood to be fixed, solid. The language that Agnes Martin used was wonderful and I am very appreciative of her art. It is majestic.

I found another message in the writing of Gertrude Stein, and especially I was attracted to her essay called "Composition as explanation". I used it to teach with and I often used sections of it in performances. She said so much that was true and clear. She was an American woman and an artist and she wrote the same clear messages that I heard from Rinpoche. The three phrases of hers that I used over and over were: "beginning again and again", "using everything", and "a continuous present". These three "mottos" became guides in the exploration of creating forms from everyday life.

Working with these messages meant changing the view of how the world was put together. It is a startling experience to unravel the way you think, and to knit a new cloth. However, when the commitment is made to work with your mind through spiritual disciplines then it is inevitable. It is quite uncomfortable and completely rigorous. And it takes a long time. Unfortunately we are often impatient when we are ready to change. We want it right now. But in this particular process it doesn't work like that.

*Photo 89: Barbara Dilley, On Concert, The Naropa-Institute, 1985
(Photo: Bill Arnold)*

4.4 Teaching Composition

When I was invited to teach at The Naropa Institute in 1974 I had never taught for a continuous length of time. I had done a lot of performances both with groups and solo. I was also beginning to make art work. I felt that by becoming a teacher I could sort through all these various experiences around creative process and figure out what was important to pass on. Some things are important to speak about and some, well, why bother.

And it was composition that seemed important to teach. Not choreography, which refers only to the making of dances, but composition, which refers to the whole spectrum of creative expression. Composition is about making something out of nothing. You start with "things as they are", ordinary movement, common objects, the everyday life and you "use everything". Creative work is meant to communicate those parts of our human experience that are intimate, sacred and often delicate aspects of our intelligence and perception.

There is a slogan from the disciplines of dharma that addresses this quality of communication. The slogan goes: "The process of exchange begins with oneself.". so when we want to exchange information with each other we must begin with ourselves. We must learn who we are and what we intend and we must know our experience. Another Slogan is "exchanging oneself with others". This asks that we reach out into the world of "other" and imagine ourselves to be them. This is a wonderful way to develop the skills for greater artistic communication.

Since I had never taught composition I thought for a long time about what would be the first assignment I would ask people to do. I wanted something that was ordinary and represented these ideas of simple communication. So I came up with the assignment "Build Me A Fire". Fires are both ordinary and not, so to speak. We have all had experiences with the magic and mystery of fire. They require us to work with the basic elements: wood, wind, space and of course, fire. This assignment would tap into each one's history of that experience with fire. They would have to think about space; where a fire could be built and what materials would burn; how long, how high, how hot, etc. there is the literal metaphor of communicating warmth. It is fundamental. I envisioned that the class would dialogue in a lively way as each person presented their assignment. People would be inspired to build more and more imaginative fires and more and more outrageously bizarre fires. First there would be the ordinary indoor fire, and then there would be the outside fire, and then there would be the fire in a teacup and the fire in the ..... whatever. As you see I could fantasize all the „compositions" that would come from having this assignment. Fires are full of the unexpected. Sometimes we can't light the match. We try match after match. And there is the quality of danger, the sparks flying around. Wood pieces jumping out of the fire. That edge is present. The possibility of getting out of control or perhaps someone will catch fire by getting to close. We can feel the direct destruction that is there. The atmosphere becomes heightened. And so we begin to study composition. In the teachings of Dharma Art there is the practice of clarifying the beginning, the middle, and the end. When we build our fire we have to create the beginning - building it. People will have to sit through its burning and perhaps someone will have to put it out. So we begin to understand the patterns and timings of this activity of building a fire from the beginning to the end.

This assignment gave people a way to approach creative awareness. We develop creative awareness through knowing the elements, the basic components of our experience - hot and cold, light and dark, wet and dry. Our perceptual awareness - sight, sound, smell, etc. - of the elements is important to relate to in composition.

I must say right now that developing awareness is not easy. When you are teaching people about awareness it is important to begin with what they already understand - with how they feel, what they perceive and how they think. You must be gentle and encouraging as you go along and there must be a sense of making friends with yourself and with what one doesn't understand, one's ignorance. Because the way to develop awareness is to recognize and understand one's ignorance - the spacing out, turning away from, and losing it - whatever it feels like when the awareness isn't happening. We all have a sense of when it is happening - and then, when it isn't. Awareness comes from appreciating those moments when there isn't any awareness, making friends with that experience, and being gentle.

Creativity and making art from our everyday lives requires us to be gentle. I have found this part to take a long time. So you have to also have a sense of humor. It is essential. You have to chuckle at yourself and even poke fun at yourself. Otherwise you'll be very boring.

4.5 Three Aspects

There are three aspects to this mingling of the two streams. - the contemporary American improvisational dance stream and the Buddhist meditation, awareness training, non-aggressive art and taming of the mind stream. These three aspects, based on Buddhist philosophy, are the disciplines that join our hearts and minds.

The first aspect is the outer aspect. It is a discipline of paying a great deal of attention to details. It means training yourself daily to pay great attention to the details of your life - in the kitchen, the bedroom, with your pocketbook, with your friends. Paying attention is a way of caring for things that fill our world. Having respect and appreciation for all parts of our daily life guides our heart and mind toward expressing a sense of sacredness to all that surrounds us.

The second aspect is the inner aspect. It is about the inner, personal world, our physical body. How we speak, how we move, the experience of living with this body, its perceptions, feelings, how it unfolds - all this we can learn to be at one with. The discipline is to practice being at one with our perceptions, at one with what we see, hear; what we taste. To be united with our sense perceptions and not vanish off somewhere. So the discipline is to bring yourself back to the experiences and expression of your body, fully and constantly.

The final aspect is the "secret" one. It expresses the transcendent awareness that comes from simultaneously attending to details without and to what is happening within. With this discipline we develop a sense of knowing what to say and how to care for ourselves. With this coming together of understanding about the environment and our actions, there is a total awakeness, or what is called "nowness". In this atmosphere of "nowness" there is ease and delight, a power. When this atmosphere of "nowness" is present, communication between you and me occurs openly and with complete appropriateness.

So the three aspects of discipline for joining our hearts and minds are, first paying attention to the details, then being there with all of it - the perception, the movements, sounds, sights, smells. And finally, when the outer world and the inner perceptions are synchronized there is this presence of "nowness". It is awake and without conflict. It is natural and open - it is direct communication.

Barbara Dilley, an american performance artist, developed "Contemplative Dance" as a connection between improvisation and Buddhistic meditation. She was for many years head of the dance department of The Naropa Instiute and now serves as Director. (The Naropa Instiute, 2130 Arapahoe Avenue, Boulder, CO 80302-6697. Tel. 001-303-546-357). Barbara Dilley also teaches in many European countries.

Bibliography

Bainbridge Cohen, Bonnie: Sensing, Feeling and Action. Contact Editions, 1993.

Bewegung Kunterbunt. Spiel und Sport für behinderte und nichtbehinderte Kinder: Sportjugend Hessen, Tips 5, 1996.

Blume, Michael: Akrobatik. Meyer & Meyer, 1992.

Charlip, Remy: First Remy Charlip Reader. Contact Editions, 1994.

Chödrön, Pema: Start were your are. Shambhala Publications, 1995.

Contact-Quarterly. A vehicle for moving ideas, 1975 - 1997.

Forti, Simone: Handbook in Motion. The Press of Nova Scotia College of Art und Design, Halifax 1974.

Halprin, Anna: Tamalpa Institute/Dancers' Workshop, 1979.

Haselbach, Barbara: Improvisation, Tanz, Bewegung. Klett, 1993.

Kaltenbrunner, Thomas: Reflexzonenmassage: Anleitung zur Eigen- und Partnermassage. Mosaik, 1994.

Kaltenbrunner, Thomas: Shiatsu – Die heilende Kraft der japanischen Massagetherapie. Mosaik, 1997.

Matt, Pamela: A Kinesthetic Legacy. The Life and Works of Barbara Clark. CMT Press, 1993.

Novack, Cynthia J.: Sharing the Dance: Contact Improvisation and American Culture. The University of Wisconsin Press, 1990.

Petzhold, H.G.: Integrative Therapie: Modelle, Theorien und Methoden für eine schulenübergreifende Psychotherapie. Band II, 3. Jungfermann, 1993.

Rolland, John: Inside Motion. Roland String Research Associates, 1987.

Trungpa, Chögyam: Cutting through Spiritual Materialism. Shambhala Publications, 1973.

Trungpa, Chögyam: Shambhala – The Sacred Path of the Warrior. Shambhala Publications, 1984.

Adresses

Adresses in Europe:

Contemplative Dance, Dharma-Art and Meditation:
Germany: Shambhala Zentrum, Wilhelmstr. 20, D-35037 Marburg, Tel.: 06421/17020

France: Shambhala Zentrum Europa, Dechen Chöling, Mas Marvant, F-87700 Saint Yrieix sous Aix, Frankreich, Tel.: 0033-55035552

EDDC, European Dance Development Center, Arnhem, Nijhoffstraat 42, 6821 BM Arnhem, Niederlande, Tel:: 00312635642 (Zweigstelle auch in Düsseldorf s.u. Die Werkstatt)

Kaltenbrunner, Thomas (FORUM), Barfüßerstr. 14, D-35037 Marburg, Tel./Fax: 06421-21194

Keriac c/o K. Azza, Lerchenstr. 69, D-70176 Stuttgart, Tel.: 0711/6369189

Newsletter (dt. Ausg.), „artblau", Bültenweg 95, D-38106 Braunschweig, Tel.: 0531-345386

Newsletter (engl. Ausg.), CONTACT CONNECTION, 37 A Cecilia Road, London E82 ER, Tel.: 0044(0)172-2492899

School für New Dance Development, Da Costakade 102, 1053 WP Amsterdam, Niederlande, Tel.: 0031/20-6833114

Adresses in USA:

Contact-Quarterly, A vehicle for moving ideas. P.O. Box 603, Northampton, MA 01060; Tel.: 001/413-586-1181

Canada: Shambhala International, 1084 Tower Road, Halifax, N.S. B3H2Y5, Tel.: 303/881-2184

USA: Karma Chöling, RR1, Box 3, Barnet, VT 05821, Tel.: 802/633-2384

Keriac, Dance Ground Studio, Postadresse: 2261 Market Street, Nr. 116; San Francisco, Ca 94114, Tel.: 415-775-5663

Naropa Institute, 2130 Arapahoe Avenue, Boulder, CO 80302-6697, Tel.: 001-303-546-3578

Tamalpa Institute (Anna Halprin), 15 Ravine Way, Kentfield, CA 94904, Tel.: 001-415-461-5362

Quotes

1. March 1977 for CBC Radio, quoted in Contact Quarterly , Vol III, No.1
2. Contact Improvisation / A Definition - Contact Quarterly, Vol II, No.4
3. Contact Quarterly Vol IV, No.2
4. Contact Quarterly Vol 111 No.1
5. Der Züricher Oberländer" from 11.11.1982 about a contact-workshop
6. From Politics and Contact - Contact Quarterly Vol VII, No.1
7. Müller / Stöckermann, "...jeder Mensch ist ein Tänzer", Anabas Verlag, 1993
8. Quoted in Novack, J. Cynthia, "Sharing the Dance". The Univerisity of Wisconsin Press, 1990
9. Seminar catalogue of the Stuttgart Volkshochschule 1996
10. Contact Quarterly Vol XIV, No.1.
11. In correspondence with the author
12. Contact Quarterly Vol II, No.1
13. Contact Quarterly Vol VII, No.3/4, 1982, p. 17
14. Contact Quarterly Vol XIV, No.1
15. Quoted in Novack, J. Cynthia, Sharing the Dance. The Univerisity of Wisconsin Press, 1990
16. Contact Quarterly - Vol. XIII No.3
17. Contact Quarterly Vol V No.3/4
18. Contact Quarterly Vol V, No.1
19. Contact Quarterly Vol XXIII, No.1
20. Sensing, Feeling and Action, Contact Editions, 1993
21. Petra Vetter in a workshop flyer, Germany 1995
22. In correspondence with the author
23. Quoted in Novack, J. Cynthia, Sharing the Dance. The Univerisity of Wisconsin Press, 1990 p.72
24. In correspondence with the author
25. In correspondence with the author
26. Contact Quarterly Vol VI, No.3/4
27. Contact Quarterly Vol XII, No.2
28. The Contact Duet as a Paradigm for Client/Therapist Interaction, Dance Therapy Program, Naropa Institute, 1988
29. Novack, J. Cynthia, Sharing the Dance. The Univerisity of Wisconsin Press, 1990
30. Novack, J. Cynthia, Sharing the Dance. The Univerisity of Wisconsin Press, 1990
31. The Drama Review - Vol. 19 No. 1 T-65, 1975
32. Contact Quarterly Vol XVI, No.1

33. Contact Quarterly Vol II, No.1

34. Quoted in Contact Quarterly Vol V, No.1

35. Translated from German: "Abschied von der Selbstzerstörung", Kreuz, 1987

36. Quoted in Workshop publicity for Barbara Dilley, 1996

37. Kaltenbrunner, Thomas, Die metaphysisch-personale Anthropologie von Karlfried Graf Dürckheim, Dissertation Albert-Ludwigs-Universität Freiburg 1997

38. Contact Quarterly Vol III, No.1

39. Contact Quarterly Vol. VII, No.3/4

40. Contact Quarterly Vol. II, No.3

41. Contact Quarterly Vol XXI, No.1

42. Contact Quarterly Vol XXI ,No.2

43. Contact Quarterly Vol XXI, No.2

44. In correspondence with the author

45. Contact Quarterly Vol III, No.1

46. Contact Quarterly Vol XXI, No.2

47. Contact Quarterly Vol II, No.3/4

48. Contact Quarterly, Vol IV, No. 1

49. Contact Quarterly Vol XVII, No.2

50. Shambala – The Sacred Path of the Warrior, Shambala Publications, Boston, 1982

51. Shambala – The Sacred Path of the Warrior, Shambala Publications, Boston, 1982

52. Contact Quarterly Vol XIV, No.2

53. In correspondence with the author

54. From workshop flyer, San Fransisco 1995

55. Quoted in Lemieux, Adwoa, The Contact Duet as a Paradigm for Client/Therapist Interaction, Dance Therapy Program, Naropa Institute, 1988

56. Workshop flyer, Boulder 1995

57. Contact Quarterly Vol XV, No.3

58. Sensing, Feeling and Action, Contact Editions, 1993

59. Quoted in Novack, J. Cynthia, Sharing the Dance. The Univerisity of Wisconsin Press, 1990

60. The Contact Duet as a Paradigm for Client/Therapist Interaction, Dance Therapy Program, Naropa Institute, 1988

61. In panel discussion, quoted in Brinkmann, Ulla, Kontaktimprovisation, Afra-Verlag, 1992

62. Quoted in Lemieux, Adwoa, The Contact Duet as a Paradigm for Client/Therapist Interaction, Dance Therapy Program, Naropa Institute, 1988

63. Quoted in Lemieux, Adwoa, The Contact Duet as a Paradigm for Client/Therapist Interaction, Dance Therapy Program, Naropa Institute, 1988

64. Action Theater, North Atlantic Books, 1995

65. Quoted in Thomas Kaltenbrunner, Reflexzonenmassage, Mosaic Verlag, 1994

66. Contact Quarterly Vol III, No.3/4

67. Lambert Schneider, Bleicher Verlag, 1997

68. Mudra, Shambhala Publications, 1972

69. Drama Review, Vol 19 No. 1, T-65, 1975

70. Contact Quarterly Vol II, No.1

71. Contact Quarterly Vol VII, No.3/4

72. Quoted in Novack, J. Cynthia, Sharing the Dance. The Univerisity of Wisconsin Press, 1990

73. Contact Quarterly Vol III, No.1

74. Contact Quarterly Vol VII, No.3/4

75. Contact Quarterly Vol II, No.2

76. Translated from Kontaktimprovisation, Afra-Verlag, 1992

77. Sharing the Dance. The Univerisity of Wisconsin Press, 1990

78. In correspondence with the author

79. Contact Quarterly Vol III, No.1

80. In correspondence with the author

81. Contact Quarterly Vol IV, No.1

82. Quoted in Novack, J. Cynthia, Sharing the Dance. The Univerisity of Wisconsin Press, 1990

83. Contact Quarterly Vol III, No.3/4

84. Quote Scott Wells - from Thomas (p.120)

85. John Dewey – Bon mot

86. Contact Quarterly Vol XVI, No.1

87. In correspondence with the author

88. Workshop flyer, 1995

89. Workshop Flyer, 1995

90. Contact Quarterly Vol II, No.1

91. In correspondence with the author

92. Contact Quarterly Vol XX, No.2

93. Contact Quarterly Vol XX, No.2

94. Contact Quarterly Vol II, No.1

95. Workshop flyer, 1996

96. Publicity material, 1992

97. Nietzsche, Friedrich. Kritische Gesamtausgabe. 8 Abt. Bergr. v. Colli, Giorgio/ Montinari, Mazzino, Fortgef. v. Müller-Lauter, Wolfgang/ Pestalozzi, Karl. 'de Gruyter

98. Body Stories, Station Hill Press, 1991

99. Quoted in Lemieux, Adwoa, The Contact Duet as a Paradigm for Client/Therapist Interaction, Dance Therapy Program, Naropa Institute, 1988

100. Contact Quarterly Vol X, No.2

101. Translated from interview in tanz aktuell, June 1990

102. In correspondence with the author

103. Action Theater, North Atlantic Books, 1995

104. In correspondence with the author

105. Contact Quarterly Vol XVIII, No.1

106. Contact Quarterly Vol II, No.1

107. In correspondence with the author

108. Workshop flyer, Germany 1993

109. Contact Quarterly Vol XX, No.2

110. Integrative Therapie, Jungfermann Verlag, 1994

English Titles
Meyer & Meyer Publishing

CSRC Edition Volume 1

Ethics, Sport and Leisure

Crisis and Critiques

Tomlinson/Fleming (eds.)

304 pages, paperback,
14,8 x 21 cm
ISBN 3-89124-441-X
£ 14.95/US$ 24.-/
Austr.$ 32.95/$NZ 36.95/
Can$ 34.95

CSRC Edition Volume 2

Education, Sport and Leisure

Mc Fee/Tomlinson (eds.)

232 pages, paperback,
14,8 x 21 cm
ISBN 3-89124-442-8
£ 12.95/US$ 17.95/
Austr.$ 28.95/$NZ 32.95/
Can$ 25.95

CSRC Edition Volume 3

Gender, Sport and Leisure

Alan Tomlinson (ed.)

272 pages, paperback,
14,8 x 21 cm
ISBN 3-89124-443-6
£ 14.95/US$ 24.-/
Austr.$ 32.95/$NZ 36.95/
Can$ 34.95

CSRC Edition Volume 4

Sport in Diveded Societies

Sugden/Bairner (eds.)

300 pages, paperback,
14,8 x 21 cm
ISBN 3-89124-445-2
£ 12.95/US$ 17.95/
Austr.$ 28.95/$NZ 32.95/
Can$ 25.95

CSRC Edition Volume 5

Sport, Popular Culture and Identity

Maurice Roche (ed.)

226 pages, paperback,
14,8 x 21 cm
ISBN 3-89124-468-1
£ 12.95/US$ 17.95/
Austr.$ 28.95/$NZ 32.95/
Can$ 25.95

CSRC Edition Volume 6

Taking Sport Seriously

Lincoln Allison (ed.)

206 pages, paperback,
14,8 x 21 cm
ISBN 3-89124-479-7
£ 14.95/US$ 17.95/
Austr.$ 28.95/$NZ 32.95/
Can$ 25.95

Information about the "CSRC-Edition"

The Chelsea School Research Centre Edition originated in the advanced scholarship and research undertaken in CSRC as it consolidated and developed its national and international research networks. It brings together state-of-the art scholarship and research in sport sociology, sport sciences, leisure studies and physical education.

Each edition will comprise multidisciplinary approaches to a common theme, or themed collections based upon single disciplines, depending upon the specific focus of the title. Specialist scholars form the CSRC or prominent authors from other universities and Research Centres are the contributors to the edition.

Modern Sports
Karate

Basics of Techniques and Tactics
Rudolf Jakhel

160 pages, 320 photos,
paperback,
14,8 x 21 cm
ISBN 3-89124-428-2
£ 12.95/US$ 17.95/
Austr.$ 28.95/$NZ 32.95/
Can$ 25.95

Scientific Coaching for Olympic Taekwondo

Pieter/Heijmans

248 pages, 90 photos,
45 figures, paperback,
14,8 x 21 cm
ISBN 3-89124-389-8,
£ 12.95/US$ 17.95/
Austr.$ 28.95/$NZ 32.95/
Can$ 25.95

Training Exercises for Competitive Tennis

Lutz Steinhöfel

176 pages, 20 photos and
figures, paperback,
14,8 x 21 cm
ISBN 3-89124-464-9
£ 12.95/US$ 17.95/
Austr.$ 28.95/$NZ 32.95/
Can$ 25.95

Running to the Top

Arthur Lydiard

184 pages, illustrations,
paperback, 14,8 x 21 cm
ISBN 3-89124-440-1,
£ 12.95/US$ 17.95/
Austr.$ 28.95/$NZ 32.95/
Can$ 25.95

Handbook for Beach Volleyball

Hömberg/Papageorgiou

296 pages, hardcover,
14,8 x 21 cm
ISBN 3-89124-322-7,
£ 17.95/US$ 29.-/
Austr.$ 37.-/$NZ 42.-/
Can$ 39.95

Handbook for Cycle Racing

Training: Keep Fit Tacti

Achim Schmidt

264 pages, 16 pages colou
paperback, 14,8 x 21 cm
ISBN 3-89124-509-2,
£ 12.95/US$ 19.95/
Austr.$ 30.95/$NZ 34.95/
Can$ 29.95

Triathlon Training

From Novice to Ironman
Hermann Aschwer

248 pages, 40 photos,
30 figures, paperback,
14,8 x 21 cm
ISBN 3-89124-515-7,
£ 12.95/US$ 19.95/
Austr.$ 30.95/$NZ 34.95/
Can$ 29.95

Straight Golf

The Basics of Good Golf
Mund/Münch

264 pages, 140 figures,
paperback,
14,8 x 21 cm
ISBN 3-89124-503-3
£ 12.95/US$ 19.95/
Austr.$ 30.95/$NZ 34.95/
Can$ 29.95

Jazz Dance Training

Dörte Wessel-
Therhorn

208 pages, 250 photos and
figures, paperback,
14,8 x 21 cm
ISBN 3-89124-499-1
£ 12.95/US$ 17.95/
Austr.$ 28.95/$NZ 32.95/
Can$ 25.95

MEYER
&MEYER
SPORTS